Ask!

ASK!

The Revolutionary New Guide for Getting Total Customer Satisfaction

Barbara Rollin

St. Martin's Griffin ≈ New York

www.stmartins.com

Book design by Ellen Cipriano

LIBRARY OF CONGRESS CATALOGING-IN-PUBLICATION DATA
Rollin, Barbara.
    Ask! the revolutionary new guide for getting total customer satisfaction /
Barbara Rollin.
        p. cm.
    Includes bibliographical references.
    ISBN 0-312-28388-1
    1. Consumer satisfaction. I. Title.

HF5415.335 .R65 2001
658.8'12—dc21

                                                                2001041810

First Edition: November 2001

10 9 8 7 6 5 4 3 2 1

This book is dedicated to my parents, Hermia and Larry Hyams, to my husband, David, and to my children, Julie, Michael, and his wife, Christina, all of whom contributed their love, support, and critical advice. And to my grandchildren, Maya and Leo, who bring me joy.

Contents

Acknowledgments

This book couldn't have been written without the encouragement, insight, and editing of my husband, David. He's also my best salesperson in his belief that *Ask!* offers real value to readers. My thanks to my daughter, Julie; my son, Michael; my parents, Hermia and Larry Hyams; and my close friend Harriett Krucoff for their editing and critical input.

A special thanks to Jane Ockershausen for believing in my writing through the years.

Thanks also to Ellen Furman, Robert Harrington, Laurie Richards, and Michael Schwager for reading drafts.

And thanks to those who shared their stories: Fred Barnett, Stel Barnett, Sharon Bradley, Rick Bradley, David Callahan, Lucy Escoffier, Trisha Gum, Jason Krucoff, David Phillips, Juliet Phillips, Gina Silverman.

I'm especially grateful to my editor, Jennifer Enderlin, who had the vision to love my book from the beginning; to her assistant, Kim Cardascia, for her clear editorial eye and forthright approach; and to my agent, Richard Curtis, for his skill, wisdom, and humor.

Disclaimer

The reader should realize that companies do change their policies and what worked for me with one company yesterday may not work for you tomorrow, even with that same company. Also, some of the companies I had trouble with may have changed their ways or I may have had the rare rotten experience. Every company has bad days. While I make no guarantees, the real lesson of this book is that no matter what problem you have as a consumer, the chances are you can and will improve your lot if you only ASK.

All names in the book are real, with the exception of those few that appear in quotes the first time they are used.

Ask!

1.

If You Don't Ask, the Answer Is Always No

But I *did* ask. In September of 1993, I bought five-year certificates of deposit at an interest rate of 5 percent. By December 1994, the rate had climbed to 6 percent. I felt foolish that I'd locked up my money for so long, and I felt trapped by the hefty penalties for early withdrawal. Then I had an idea. Would it hurt to call the banks and ask them to raise my rate? It was probably a waste of time, but **I had nothing to lose.**

There were five institutions in all. First I called the one where I had the most money. I spoke with a supervisor and simply asked, "Can you help me? The rates have gone up since I purchased my CDs. Could you raise my rate?"

The woman said she'd have to consult her supervisor. After a few minutes she came back on the line. "We'd be glad to do that," she said.

Just like that. They raised my rate from 5.61 percent to 6.35 percent *because I asked.* I didn't have to tell them a hard luck story, or plead, or threaten, or beg. I just asked. Astonishing. Up until now, I'd imagined banks to be impenetrable monoliths, as I did other large institutions.

Two months later, in February 1995, the rates went up

another percent. I asked again. Again they said "yes." This time they raised my rate from 6.35 percent to 7.08 percent.

I had similar results with three of the five institutions I asked. The last two said no, "no" as in, "are you out of your mind?" But that was the response I'd *expected*. It was lucky that I got a "yes" from the first institution or I might not have persevered.

These few phone calls resulted in a net gain of $10,000 over five years. But I gained more than money. I got psychological relief from my feelings of being foolish and trapped. I felt good instead of bad. This was a pure example of an Ask. It wasn't a complaint or a grievance. It was simply a request for help in bettering my situation.

The lesson I learned was—**if you don't ask, the answer is always no.** There's nothing too outrageous to ask for. You're entitled to ask for anything. You're not always going to get a positive answer. But you *are* entitled to ask.

Ask! is about asking the unaskable to get what you need and deserve. It's about conditioning ourselves to question everything—to question tradition, habit, and custom. Not to make assumptions or take anything as a given. Not to automatically take no for an answer.

That's how I convinced a bank to reverse itself and approve a mortgage, received replacement costs of $720 on a comforter ruined by a dry cleaner, persuaded a lawyer to refund half her fee, returned prescription drugs, had charges waived—from credit card annual fees to airline change fees. It's how I collected more than $800 in bonuses in one year from long-distance phone companies, got reimbursed for wasted time by retailers, obtained all sorts of things *for free*—from discontinued merchandise to referral fees—**that are available to everyone.** But you have to Ask.

We, as individual consumers, feel helpless in the face of the powerful companies we inevitably deal with daily. We've been socialized to believe we have no power. It's difficult to step back and ask questions, to stop ourselves from responding in habitual ways. It takes energy. Asking goes counter to everything we've been taught. We've internalized such parental injunctions as "don't question authority," "be polite," "go with the flow," "don't make waves," and sadly, "half a loaf is better than none." These internalized messages, according to psychologists, create a sense of "learned helplessness," one of the main causes of depression.[1] The fact is we *have* power and don't realize it. *Ask!* is about using the power we already have.

None of us is immune to the hassles of everyday life. And since we don't produce any part of the vast assortment of goods we consume, there's no avoiding these hassles. We must constantly interact with the commercial world. With banks, landlords, airlines, hotels, car dealers, repair shops, rentals, lawyers. We have to contend with defective items, dry cleaners, long-distance phone services, shrinking garments, discontinued styles, disappointing restaurant dinners, delivery and repair people who don't show up on time, undisclosed surcharges, unadvertised discounts, unhonored warranties—and new challenges that are continually being imposed on us by the marketplace such as "risk management departments," "restocking fees," "presales," corporate mergers, large rebate offers, huge grocery stores housing franchised vendors like banks, photo developers, dry cleaners, specialty foods.

These hassles occupy more space in our brains than the important things. They negatively affect our quality of life by gobbling up energy that could be used for more fulfilling activities. Since there's no escaping these hassles, I've come up with techniques to handle them that are effective, empowering, easy to implement, and even fun. Sometimes, in fact, you can turn an aggravation into an opportunity. Like what happened when I was the not-so-proud owner of too many low-interest CDs.

This is *not* a book about complaining, but rather about Asking. Complaining takes a psychological toll. When you complain, you cringe at the sound of your own voice with its petulant whine of entitlement. Inherent in complaining is the anticipation of getting screwed, which becomes a self-fulfilling prophecy. You block the help that might otherwise be available.

In contrast to complaining—and I can whine with the best—Asking avoids creating adversarial situations. I've gotten my best results by staying human and treating other people like humans also, not holding them responsible for a bum product (the stalled traffic, or, you fill-in-the-blanks). By staying human, you have the chance to make a real human contact that can effectively humanize a large corporation. Dealing with *individuals* within a corporation is far different from dealing with corporate behavior. Almost certainly, an injustice coming from a business is *not* the fault of the person at the other end of the line. The individual may be as oppressed by the corporation as you are.

Asking *feels* better than complaining. It's more humane and psychologically healthier. And even if you don't get what you've asked for, you won't become agitated, shamed, or infuriated because you've remained calm and polite. Your day won't be ruined. You won't get into a black mood and need to vent on those you *are* in personal relationships with. It's amazing how it works, but if you don't lose your dignity with others, you'll be able to respect yourself.

This approach hasn't come naturally to me. I'm from New York—City, that is. When I moved to Maryland in 1966, it took three years for my face to thaw. At first, when the checkout clerk in the supermarket asked how I was, it took me a minute to recover. (Back then, New York lived up to its hard-boiled reputation. *No one* in a supermarket was concerned with how you were. Supermarkets were dangerous places where you could sustain permanent injuries from recklessly driven shopping carts.)

Because of my New York background, when I go to make a call, I have to lecture myself to remain calm. I have to remind myself that the minute my voice rises, I can count on an interaction going awry. I've had to train myself to stay polite, to treat the person at the other end of the line like a human being (despite all evidence to the contrary).

My successes and those of my family and friends have enabled me to turn up the volume on Asking. Each success emboldens me further. These victories, large and small, give us a sense that there *is* some justice in the world.

Sometimes things fall in my lap—I often receive more than I'd hoped for. There are no longer occasions when I kick myself for *not* asking. And I'm not afraid of the word "aggressive." It's a term used to manipulate us into settling for less.

This book has no legal advice. It addresses the normal irritations of everyday life for which most of us would never think to seek legal redress: the gap between pursuing litigation and throwing a defective item into the garbage. It can range from asking the seemingly impossible—and getting more than you ever imagined—to simply asking to be treated fairly. You have nothing to lose. And we all have different priorities. What's deplorable negligence to one person is unimportant to another.

Ask! is both a practical approach for handling everyday aggravations and a bold assault on the system. Some of my stories will shock you. *She has some nerve,* you'll think. *How could she?*

Where does she get off? You'll question if this is the correct way to act. I've had to wrestle with these issues, too. Is this a legitimate way to behave? I've asked myself. Is it, in fact, nice?

What I've realized is, we confuse behavior appropriate for commercial situations with behavior appropriate in personal relationships. Businesses know this. **They're counting on it.** So although *they* do not apply the standards of interpersonal relationships to us, they're confident we're thoroughly conditioned to applying these standards to them. They know we like to think of ourselves as "nice" people.

The fact that we sense something's askew in this relationship is reflected in the cynicism of the oft-expressed rhetorical question, What can you expect from business? We're cynical about business practices, yet we feel uncomfortable applying *their* standards to *them.*

So if you're outraged or embarrassed by things you read in this book, ask yourself if you're judging my actions by the standards of "polite society." This is *not* a book about interacting with friends, family, or even an *individual* within a corporation. Consider that nothing in this book is either illegal or immoral or even unkind.

In the last century, the structure of commerce has gone from the neighborhood store, whose owner had a face, to huge, faceless, multifaceted conglomerates. This means that most of our everyday activities involve asymmetrical relationships where the company has the power to manipulate. They have business consultants to advise them on what products will appeal and how to market them. They have expert psychological data predicting our minutest moves, like whether we'll turn left or right when we enter a department store.[2] They know how to make us believe that an item of clothing we loved last year is now distasteful, "out of fashion," dated. I pride myself on having a fashion-free wardrobe; yet there I am, looking at last-year's sweater, and thinking how shapeless it is, how this year's tops look "better." How could I have worn that? The shoulder pads are too big. I look like a football player. And the color!

As *Consumer Reports* points out in its September 2000 edition, "No part of the shopping experience happens by accident." Did you know that items featured in "sale" flyers—which *CR* says are glanced at by 80 percent of shoppers—are often not on sale at all, or discounted only by pennies? No? Me neither. "Grocery manufacturers," *Consumer Reports* notes, "pay handsomely to get their products mentioned in flyers and newspaper ads: A mention, even if it's not accompanied by a discount, can boost sales."[3] Deceptive? Possibly. But definitely intentionally misleading.

Since dealing with large corporations is a relatively recent phenomenon, it's not surprising we haven't sorted out an appropriate code of behavior to interface with business. In fact, we haven't even been aware of the *need* for such a code.

We're confused. That's because we've succumbed to our conditioning. Our confusion stems from the fact that the traits essential to being a successful consumer are behaviors you *don't* want to practice in interpersonal relationships, where they'd be inappropriate or even destructive. Like persistence. Persistence is an important tool in dealing with business, yet try using it on your spouse and you may need persistence in finding your *next* mate. And bypassing—bypassing an underling to talk with a supervisor. (Your husband's mother?) In *Ask!,* I've come up with ways to remain human, polite, yet address our rights.

Ask! is different from anything you've ever read. It's a survival guide for successfully navigating the system. I share my strategies for achieving terrific results, often immediately, that will help you gain more control of your life. And there're enough ideas to earn you back the price of the book many times over.

Asking is a way for every individual to feel empowered. You don't need advanced degrees or fat purses. It's a practical approach that can be used by anyone. There are no age, sex, educational, or financial restrictions. The most important thing is to have a good attitude and an understanding that you *do* have power. My best tool is my attitude—that everything is open to question and negotiation. *Everything.*

The stories that follow are examples of situations where Asking is possible; examples, because they'll help you reframe your approach to everyday aggravations in your *own* life. Irritations will begin to seem like opportunities. You don't have to make any major changes in your personality to implement the techniques of *Ask!* but using these techniques *will* help you psychologically.

As for life's larger troubles, in the final section I look at how to use the principles of *Ask!* to obtain the best possible medical care.

How did this book get written? My new husband, a cognitive scientist who studies the way we think, overheard my phone conversations with airlines, repair people, department stores, banks, and the like. The results amazed him.

"You know," he said, "you handle things very differently. You should write about it. It would help people."

"Naaaaah," I said—I was busy writing short stories.

A few days later, after listening to another conversation that ended with yet another spectacular outcome, he repeated his suggestion and added, "Why don't you take just fifteen minutes a day and write up some of your consumer victories? Your style is unique."

"Okay, okay," I said, "fifteen minutes I can do."

In a month, I had five thousand words. In two months, it grew to ten thousand. Then the book wrote itself. New incidents kept popping up, remembrances of things past, stories people told me when they heard about what I was writing. I added research and interviews and *Ask!* was born.

During the past few years, I've had an eventful life. I moved four times: twice in the Washington, D.C., area, twice in San Diego. I became a grandmother of twins, I met Mr. Right, got married, we bought a house. Along with marrying Mr. Right, I married his nonagenarian parents, helped my husband move *them* twice, once to an assisted-living facility and then to a nursing home. And I helped with my new father-in-law's final illness and death. In the midst of it all, we took a three-week trip to France.

Lots of activity, lots of complicated transactions, lots of opportunities for asking.

2.
Asking—
The Hows and Whys

In the Beginning

I started out small, never imagining I'd become a Master Asker. Thirty years ago I bit down on a cherry pit in a Sara Lee turnover and wrote to the president of the company. I received a letter of apology, a gift box filled with Sara Lee goodies, and coupons for more goodies. I persuaded B. Altman's, a fancy, New York department store, to send reimbursement for a defective man's suit. The suit was charcoal gray with red and blue threads running through it. After a year of wear, the red threads had snapped and unraveled. Because I didn't have a receipt, I received only the last sale price, but that was a major victory. In those days it was rare to succeed in returning *anything*. If you convinced a store to take something back, you earned a ticker-tape parade down Wall Street.

Sometimes I hit walls. Discount stores like Loehmann's were implacable in their refusal to accommodate me. Airlines weren't much better. I was easily intimidated and dissuaded. I could take the *first* step—I was always good at that—but going further was often too much of a leap.

Back then I wrote letters. Calls were expensive—you could get an ulcer waiting on hold; it was worse than being in a taxi during a traffic jam. Long-distance calls were reserved for Sunday morning catch-ups with your parents. So when I felt like I'd gotten a raw deal, I laboriously cranked out messy, amateurish letters on a manual typewriter, carbon papers, erasable bond paper.

Letter writing was torture, but the only possible method. After much stalling, I'd force myself to write the letter, then muster the patience to wait for an answer. It took persistence writing to the head of a company—I used to run to the library and look up the names and addresses of CEOs in *Dun & Bradstreet*.

But I was one of the minority. Most people only *think* about writing. They never actually do it. Many eloquent letters get written in people's heads just before they fall asleep or shortly after they wake up. Long walks and drives are also good times for head-letter-writing. Most never write the letter, and there were many *I* didn't write.

And getting a simple refund used to be enough. I'd be grateful for a positive response even if they were table scraps. So I'd settle for reimbursement on a defective product, but not the damage it caused. I no longer do that. These days I get reimbursed for the time I've wasted *and* the damage, besides the cost of the product.

The Times They Are A-changin'

Today, the redress process is available to everyone. Businesses are more responsive, long-distance calls are cheap, or, with 800 numbers, free. Writing and creating a paper trail is important if you're planning to sue, but that's not what this book is about. I've never had to go to court. Calling ranks far above letter writing for me. It's immediate—patience not being my strong suit—and you have a chance of making a human contact. You can climb the chain of command in minutes and get quick results. AT&T says that "86 percent of customers would rather call a toll-free number than write a letter to a company, and 62 percent are more likely to do business with companies having toll-free lines than those who do not."[1]

E-mail is a convenient middle ground between calling and writing. My young friend Jason's been getting excellent results E-mailing Customer Service departments. Being thirty years old, he's comfortable using E-mail rather than writing formal letters. The E-mail addresses are on the companies' home pages.

He used E-mail to resolve a problem with Timex watches.

Date: 23 Sept 1998
Subject: Problem with 100-Lap Ironman Watch
To: custserv@timex.com

Sir or Madam:

I'm E-mailing you about a serious product defect with your 100-Lap Ironman Triathalon watch (model number 721-70381). I'm a competitive swimmer on a Master's swim team in Rockville, Maryland. The 100-Lap Ironman Triathalon watch is one of the few watches that can accommodate a full swim practice. I press the interval timer button a few hundred times per week. Unfortunately, my experiences with the watch, and specifically, the timer button, have been disappointing. I first purchased a 100-Lap Ironman watch in 1995. In less than two years, the interval timer button broke off of the watch.

Assuming that this defect was a one-time occurrence, I purchased the same model in 1997. During a swim practice last week, the same thing happened again. I feel that Timex should repair or replace my watch at no cost, including shipping. I grew up thinking that a Timex watch "takes a licking . . . keeps on ticking."

Thank you for your assistance,
Jason K

Jason E-mailed me the resolution:

Barbara:

After Timex received my E-mail, they asked me to send both watches to their return department. A few weeks later, two new watches showed up in my mailbox.

Jason

Others are also finding E-mail an effective way to address problems. An article in the travel section of the *New York Times* says that complaints about air travel to the Department of Transportation have "doubled from 1998 to 1999, rising to 20,495 from 9,608," electronic mail being the main factor in the rise. "Instead of having to write, copy and address and find a stamp, disaffected consumers can send their grievances by clicking a mouse."[2] For those who'd rather write than call, E-mail is less intimidating than letter writing because of its casual nature, its immediacy.

A book on the subject of E-mail language, *Wired Style*[3]—the Internet version of *The Chicago Manual of Style*—talks about the informality of E-mail. The Internet, it says, has created "a written dialect in which punctuation is abandoned, uppercasing is largely unknown (unless you're shouting) and all sorts of acronyms replace phrases. . . . spelling and punctuation are loose and playful. . . . Write the way people talk," the authors advise. "Don't insist on 'standard' English. Appreciate unruliness. Welcome inconsistency."

There are those who *do* enjoy writing letters. An article in the *San Diego Union-Tribune* tells of Brandon Cornett who gets a kick out of writing silly letters to companies. In fact, he's published a book about silly letter writing. He wrote to Nabisco "suggesting that the firm add to its popular Fig Newton line of products by producing 'Beef Newton.' It should be made, Cornett proposed with 'Beef (Grade A if possible), Curry powder, Frankincense (Swiss variety), pickle slather and mild vegetable slag."[4] (Cornett is stationed aboard a destroyer. I guess that explains it.)

Nabisco actually responded. "As you might expect," they wrote, "Nabisco routinely receives many ideas, suggestions, and new product concepts from enthusiastic consumers like yourself. As I'm sure you can understand, it is not possible to consider them all."[5]

What a waste. Think of all Cornett could accomplish with that letter-writing energy. What *is* interesting about this strange hobby, are the responses he elicits—a reminder that companies are **listening.** For God's sake, they even listen and respond to drivel!

The article goes on to say that "the responses can be just as startling because some of the corporations tread so carefully in crafting them. Apparently they want to make certain they don't offend a customer—no matter how bizarre that customer may appear."[6]

If companies take the trouble to read and respond to kooky letters, imagine the impact of a *real* letter.

Web Site

Visit the *Ask!* web site at *www.askexchange.com* to read the latest *Ask,* post your own Ask, and Ask for help with your consumer questions.

3.
Finding Help Within the System

With businesses being more responsive, it's not surprising the amount of help that's available if we approach them without hostility. Traditionally, our default position for handling consumer problems has been adversarial. A kinder, gentler, and *effective* way is to simply ask for help.

I don't believe business is trying to screw us. What business is trying to do is make money, and smart businesses are realizing that keeping the customer happy has a positive effect on the bottom line. We just have to assist them in understanding how. The old saying, "It's the squeaky wheel that gets the grease," applies even more today than it ever did. A lone voice at a responsible merchant is heard. This means that one voice represents many. It's estimated, in fact, that only one in a hundred dissatisfied customers speak up. The other ninety-nine take their business elsewhere.

Research has shown that customers who speak up are often the best customers. In the book, *A Complaint Is a Gift,* management consultants, Janelle Barlow and Claus Møller cite a study by the Technical Assistance Research Program (TARP), which, according to the authors is "the most widely quoted research group" addressing customer problems. The study claims that *"those who complain may become the most loyal customers.* They are more likely to tell their inner circle how pleased they are that the company addressed their complaint, *even if the problem was not resolved to their liking.* (Italics mine.) If the problem is resolved satisfactorily, they will tell even more people about the successful resolution of their problem than if they had received good service in the first place. . . . A company actually has a chance of increasing positive word-of-mouth advertising if it recovers for dissatisfied customers."[1]

This is an incredible plus for the consumer. Businesses are realizing that our comments are significant. We should be listened to.

Barlow and Møller go on to say that "Bain & Company, the Boston-based consulting group, estimates that profits can be boosted 25 to 95 percent—from just a 5 percent decrease in customer defection rates. What easier way to retain customers than by better handling of customer complaints?"[2]

An IBM study "suggests that if customers are left with an unresolved problem, less than half say they will repurchase. On the other hand, if customers feel that problems have been satisfactorily resolved, almost all say they will give the company another chance." For IBM, "every percentage-point variation in customer satisfaction scores translates into a gain or loss of $500 million in sales over five years. . . . developing new business costs IBM three to five times as much as selling to their existing customers."[3]

And the trend is toward even more responsiveness to customer concerns.

Because of these findings and my own experience, I encourage giving business the benefit of the doubt, not getting your dukes up. And *Ask!* isn't about complaining; it's about asking— for help, information, refunds, reimbursement, reductions, rebates. "I wonder if you can *help* me," is my mantra. Look at the titles of books about complaining—*Fight Back, and Don't Get Ripped Off,*[4] *Shocked, Appalled, and Dismayed,*[5] *Consumer Terrorism: How to Wage War against Bad Products and Worse Service,*[6] *Complaint Letters for Busy People.*[7] The titles alone express a paranoid attitude that won't contribute to successful resolution of a problem and may actually prevent it. And I learned from interviewing individuals on the other side of the customer-service interface, that my method is beneficial to both sides.

A Sticky Wicker

It's far more effective to enlist the help of someone within a company rather than rouse their anger. And if you approach service people in a friendly, nonwhining way, you'll often get far more help than you ever hoped for. That's what happened in Pier 1 Imports. I'd been eyeing a pair of wicker armchairs, but the chairs weren't on sale. And because of my deep belief in not paying full price, I asked the manager when the chairs *would* go on sale.

"Not till June," she said. "Chairs and couches go on sale in June." It was November and we needed the chairs now. The best I could do was get 10 percent off by opening a Pier 1 charge account.

The day after Christmas, we were back at Pier 1 looking at bookcases. I gasped when I saw our chairs at 40 percent off! June! If I'd known, I would have waited. Mentally, I girded myself up. I would call the national offices, tell them I'd been misinformed . . . yadda, yadda.

The manager came over to us. "How are you doing?" she asked.

"Not so well," I said. "The chairs we bought a month ago are on sale for 40 percent off."

"No problem," she said. "Just bring in your receipt and we'll credit your account."

I'd forgotten. All I had to do was Ask.

SO:

- If you don't need something right away, ask when it will go on sale.
- You don't have to rant and rave to get what you need; you just have to Ask.
- Even on large items like furniture and appliances, you might receive a refund if an item goes on sale after you bought it.

Can You Repair It
for Me Wholesale?

Right up there with life's stressful situations, like sickness and death, are car repairs—at least for me. Is it the thought of being stranded without a car? The feeling of helplessness at the hands of the repair people?

The truth is, we're not so helpless. From my daughter I learned you can negotiate with car repair shops.

"Can you help me out?" is a good way of asking. Usually, they'll drop the price by 20 percent—a reflection of how much padding there is.

Ask again. "Pleeeeese, it's such a big bill." Sometimes this will evoke a further reduction.

My Toyota Camry was just out of it's thirty-six-month warranty when the heating and air-conditioning panel conked out. It would be $500 to replace. Oh, m'God. I rifled through my repair orders and found an obscure reference to a heating system malfunction while the car was still under warranty. I brought it to the dealership and showed it to the service manager.

"I have all my repairs done here," I said. "I *did* mention that one of the buttons on the heating panel was sticking. Five hundred dollars is a lot right now. Can you help me out?"

The service manager gave me a new panel at no charge.

SO:

- You can negotiate with auto repair shops. If you ask instead of whine, you'll be delighted with the results.
- Don't assume that because a warranty is up, you're out of luck. Rules are meant to be bent. If there were related problems during the warranty period, you should ask them to fix the current problem under the expired warranty. If the new problem is just a different symptom of the old, they will likely honor the warranty.
- You'll get better results if you're a previous customer.

It's Not Us, It's You

Sometimes we have to bump up a level or two to get the help we need. My two-week-old Nissan Altima emitted hideous, grinding sounds at unpredictable times, scaring the hell out of me. These noises would emerge both when I was speeding down the highway or crawling in traffic, and sound like the engine had taken a hike.

But evidently, there are some noises that can only be heard by certain groups—namely customers—and that those very noises cannot be heard by other groups—i.e., repair people. The latter group, in fact, is so adamant about the nonexistence of these noises that they generously offer free psychiatric counseling and diagnosis; you're suffering from a well-known disorder called CND or Customer Noise Delusion.

On the first trip to the dealer, the mechanic said he couldn't hear anything, and there was nothing wrong with the car. The second visit got me a ride with the service manager. Of course, the car was perfectly behaved, making none of its scary noises. On top of it all, the service manager patronized me and told me that "nothing in life is perfect." This advice was of little use. His attitude said, "It's you, lady, not the car."

. I asked him to keep the car for testing and give me a loaner car. I could feel free to leave the car, he said, but no loaner car. And since being carless for me is right up there with the Big Ones, I thought I'd try another tack. I wrote to Nissan service. This was a few years ago. Today, I simply would have called. It would have been quicker.

September 23, 1997
Nissan Motor Corporation U.S.A.
Consumer Affairs Department
P. O. Box 191
Gardena, CA 90248-0191

Dear Sirs:

Please Help! I purchased a new Altima in May of 1997 from a dealership in Maryland. I replaced a 1989 Toyota Camry which I'd owned since it was new, and on the recommendation of friends and the reports in car magazines, decided to try an Altima.

After driving the car for two weeks, a series of noises began appearing randomly, all on the driver's side of the engine. They range from sounding as if a stiff wind is blowing under the car, metal rubbing against metal, a belt wearing out, rubbing and whirring noises. I have taken the car back to the dealer twice, and no one seems to be able to hear the noises. I was treated as if I were being overpicky. The service manager told me that the Altima is not the quietest of cars and that's just how it is. But the three friends who urged me to purchase an Altima and who own one themselves, Arlene, Jane, and Estelle, are astonished by the noises, which make the car sound like an old heap. They said that their Altimas do not make these noises, and it sounds like there's something very wrong. So I'm concluding that these noises can only be heard by middle-aged females—four of us now, not including the non-Altima owners who have been passengers—and not heard by young male mechanics. I was told to bring the car back when it does it again. I have neither the time nor the leisure to be constantly bringing the car in, especially since the service manager expressed his unwillingness to give me a loaner car. When I was going on a two-week vacation, I suggested leaving the car at the dealers, but the service manager said he "didn't see the point."

I purchased a new car because reliability is very important to me. I never had a problem with my Toyota for the seven and a half years I owned it. When I expressed my concerns about the reliability of my sick-sounding Altima to the service manager, he gave me a glib little lecture about how there are no guarantees in life. Not very reassuring. I am tired and embarrassed driving around in this weird-sounding car. I hope that you will intervene and get my car fixed. I am depending upon your excellent reputation in this matter.

Thank you,

Barbara Rollin

After two weeks, I received a call from a skilled handler of customer relations. He told me this was not the first complaint he'd received about this dealership. He couldn't understand their attitude, he said. He recommended another Nissan dealer a few minutes farther away.

In the meantime, for this problem, he contacted the old dealer and told them to give me a free loaner car and keep my car for as long as it took for them to diagnose the problem. What was important was that he took *my* side, validated my complaint, and then set about to help me resolve it. His handling of the situation retained me as a Nissan customer. In fact, it was thanks to me that my husband bought his Maxima.

But back to the uncooperative dealership. The attitude with which I was *now* greeted was vastly altered. I was treated as an honored guest. The service manager said he would have a "master" mechanic work on my car. (Who, I wondered, had worked on it before? An intern?)

The "master" discovered that two pieces of metal were rubbing against each other under the hood and, with a little twist, he separated them. Three years later the noise hasn't returned.

Conclusion: it wasn't me, it was *them.*

A version of the preceding story happened recently. Another new car. A wind whistle in the moon roof. The lecture by the salesman that nothing in life is perfect. And no, no loaner car while they investigated the problem. This time I called, instead of wrote. I called the Toyota 800 number. Customer service apologized for the salesman's attitude and said they'd be happy to pay for a rental car if the repair took more than one day. *That* I could live with.

The call took seven minutes.

SO:

+ Be persistent.
+ If you can't get satisfaction at one level, climb the ladder.
+ Don't be intimidated by the "it's not us, it's you" tactic.

The Customer
Isn't Always Wrong

I moved a lot during the past two years, lived in two apartments in Maryland and two in San Diego (my friends were beginning to wonder if I was fleeing bill collectors, but they were reassured that I still had a listed phone number) and became a connoisseur of management styles—the good, the bad, and the ugly. I experienced two very different styles: a customer-friendly, how-can-we-help-you approach and a "go away, you bother me" style. I witnessed the consequences of bad management and enjoyed the benefits of good.

In two of the apartment complexes, both advertised as luxury buildings, it felt like the personnel were trained to shake their heads no whenever a tenant neared: their heads goggling from side to side like dashboard dummies. It was no to everything. The attitude was the opposite in the two other complexes. Two out of four ain't bad—probably two more than I would have found twenty years ago.

At one of the baddies, there wasn't enough hot water. In addition to icy showers, the water in the dishwasher was cold and the dishes dirty.

"Do you rinse off your dishes before putting them in the

dishwasher?" they asked. The "it's not us, it's you" tactic again—
to put you on the defensive, shame you, make you think it's your
fault. No, I haven't lived with dishwashers my entire life; I've
been living in the jungle rubbing down my dishes with leaves so I
don't understand it's necessary to make sure the dishes are *clean*
before putting them in the dishwasher.

There was nothing wrong, they said. Then they added the
killer words, "No one else has ever complained before." Don't
you believe it. This is another tactic used to get you to shut up. It
once worked on *me*.

I've come up with effective responses to the "no one has
ever" objection.

"You know, I'm sure that's true," I say. "Studies have shown
that people *don't* complain; they just don't renew their leases."

Or I say good humoredly, "Well then, I have the distinction
of being the first," or, "Then I'm glad I got to you early so you
can fix it before you have an avalanche of complaints."

People are so baffled by these responses, they generally accommodate you.

But back to the cold water problem. Finally, a technician discovered that the hot water heater was malfunctioning. Yes, they
admitted, something *was* broken. They muttered apologies. I
noted I'd been inconvenienced for months and would like to be
compensated. They sent me a check for $250.

In the other baddy, I ran into problems immediately. There
was no phone jack in the master bedroom. When I asked the
manager to have one installed, she refused. "County regulations
call for only one jack per apartment," she informed me.

"County regulations," the "law," "company policy,"—more
words to manipulate and discourage you. "No" was an answer I
wasn't taking.

"In a luxury complex," I said, "you expect more than minimal standards. It'll be easy to run a wire from the outlet in the living room."

A half hour, in fact, was all it took, and I had a phone next to my bed.

In both of the baddies, there was a constant turnover of employees. Every time I went to the office—and it was frequent—there was a new face behind the desk.

When I asked management to intercede in convincing my upstair's neighbor to lower his stereo, they refused. The neighbor "had a right to enjoy his music," I was told. Why wasn't *I* allowed to enjoy my quiet? When did noise become a priority over quiet?

They suggested *I* contact the neighbor. The first time I called him, he apologized and adjusted the volume; but the next time, he blew up, screamed, and cursed. He said that for $1,300 a month, he would play his music when he wanted to. Then he stomped his feet and crashed into walls. Management didn't see it as their duty to intervene or admit that the tenant had gotten out of control. The division head offered me a top-floor apartment at an increase in rent of $165, moving costs to be borne by me. His offer would have been comical, but I had lost my sense of humor. Poolside, other neighbors recounted similar problems. Some had capitulated and moved to top-floor apartments at higher rents.

The only positive result of this frustrating exchange was that they offered to let me out of my lease without penalty. Even vacating, though, didn't free me of their underhandedness. They tried to keep half my security deposit for "painting, cleaning, and rug shampooing." Since I'd left the place in the same condition as when I moved in, I called to object.

"It's standard," they said. When I reread the lease, though, I found no mention of these "standard" charges. I called again.

"Normal wear-and-tear is *standard*," I said, and asked for a total refund.

"Okay," they said. Just like that.

What was standard, as I found out from other tenants, was that management withheld money from *every* security deposit, figuring that some of the vacating tenants wouldn't protest or even notice.

None of this is news. Hostile landlords are as old as time. What *is* news is that things are changing for the better. Businesses are discovering that it's good business to be responsive to the customer. You *can* find help within the system. The attitude of management in the new apartment was "How can we help you?"

A similar mishap occurred in both complexes but the way it was handled highlights the differences in their attitudes. Shortly after I moved into the "baddie," I noticed rust stains on my laundry. It took me awhile to realize the stains were coming from a rusty drum in the washing machine.

When I brought the problem to the front office, I got the usual, "You're the first . . . ," "No one else has ever . . ." They eventually replaced the machine with a reconditioned one, but they had worn me down so I never thought to ask to be reimbursed for my ruined laundry.

In the new complex, brown stains appeared on expensive, new sheets. A repairman determined that a melting rubber gasket in the dryer was the cause. *This* manager was extremely apologetic and had both a new washer and a new dryer installed.

"What about the damaged sheets?" I asked.

"No problem," she said. "Bring us a receipt and we'll take it off next month's rent." *Two hundred and fifty dollars in high-count cotton sheets.*

I told her how impressed I was with their very different

attitude. "Kathy," who had worked for the other kind of management—the negative head gogglers—agreed with me. The reason for her helpful attitude was that this management company, one of the largest in the country, had realized that the cost of training new employees far outweighed the cost of retaining productive employees, and in the current tight labor market, qualified applicants were scarce. That's why the same faces greeted me when I went to the management office, unlike in the last complex, where there were new faces every time.

Now here's what made this complex so tenant friendly. Besides the obvious ways of keeping employees happy—salary and benefits—this company learned from market research that employees are happiest when they can: make decisions, have some discretion, be empowered to say yes.

According to Kathy, "Management found you're only happy in your workplace if you have some power, some control. If you keep telling people no, it bothers you and you get really upset and eventually you leave your job. It's much easier saying yes because the employee feels better, the resident feels better." In other words, this company finds it profitable to be customer-friendly.

They keep their employees happy by both giving them power *and* training them as to how to use that power. "They put us through a very strong training process," she told me. "They do a lot of role playing. They give you the dialogue on what to say, how to phrase it, how to feel comfortable phrasing it. We take a training class at least once a month. There're very common situations that happen a lot here, so if you've got the right answers you know what you can and can't say. And they're very generous; they'll pay for any course or seminar you want to go to."

Other companies could take a few lessons from this company.

"They put a lot of emphasis on getting us not to take things personally. Just the other day we had an incident with an NSF check (insufficient funds). After two times you have to get a cashiers' check, and the girl argued and I argued and we went back and forth. The manager called and said, 'Why are you arguing? What does it matter to you? If they write a bad check, they just have to pay the NSF fee. So why are you getting so upset?'

"And so hearing that, I realize I've taken it personally when I didn't need to. They're not writing *me* an NSF check. It's like you'll bend over backward for someone, and then something will go wrong in their apartment and they'll yell at you and raise their voice and say mean things; but I tell myself, he's not mad at me, he has nothing against me, he still likes me. He'll say hi to me next week in the parking lot, but right this minute he doesn't have hot water. So management is telling me to let it go. Just let it go."

This company gives their employees power *and* psychological training.

When I told her the story of my noisy neighbor and how it was handled, she said there had been a similar situation here, but their handling of it was entirely different. They first asked the music player to raise his speakers off the floor and place them on shelves—*which management provided*. When this didn't help, the complaining tenants were given another apartment—a more expensive one on the top floor at *no extra charge*.

"They were being inconvenienced enough by moving; we didn't think we should charge them more."

"So it sounds like keeping tenants happy is important to your company?"

"Yes. The turnover rate is more expensive than keeping people happy and keeping them here. You can have someone come in at a higher rent, but you have to clean and upgrade the apartment, and the cost of doing that and the cost of advertising doesn't outweigh keeping a good tenant.

"It's come a long way, it really has changed. They do market surveys that tell them what works, what doesn't, what people like to hear, what they don't like to hear. They started this new program . . . they put out these little card flyers that say is there anything in your apartment that we can fix? A lot of people called and said, 'Well thanks for asking, but there isn't anything wrong.' They felt like we cared.

"Before this, people would come into our leasing office and say well this has been broken for two months. It's never been fixed. 'Did you ever give us a chance to fix it?' you ask them. Obviously not, they're so mad now; whereas if you contact the people, then they have no reason to be mad because nothing's built up."

This large management company believes it's good business to give good service. It's good business to empower their employees, so that they don't have to be negative head gogglers. It improves employee retention and customer contentment.

Keeping employees happy seems to have other benefits. Southwest Airlines, regarded as one of the one hundred best companies to work for by both *Fortune* magazine and San Francisco's Great Place to Work Institute, has the lowest rate of fatalities in the airline industry since 1970.[8] Keeping employees happy may be good for your health.

SO:

  - You can find help right there within the system. Businesses
    are realizing that it's good business to keep the customer
    happy.

- Don't be intimidated by phrases like "Nobody has ever complained about this before," "You're the first to complain," "company policy," "the law," "county regulations," or "that's standard." Agree with them and repeat your problem.
- Persist.
- Quiet is a right as much as someone's playing loud music. (More, as far as I'm concerned.)
- You're entitled to be compensated for inconvenience and damage caused by an apartment complex's negligence.
- Question charges that don't look right. Read your lease.
- Before you rent, research management policies. Find a place where they believe it's good business to keep the customer satisfied.

4.

Starting Out Easy

This section is about easy Asks. You just have to ask. You don't have to beg, wheedle, whine, rant, stomp, yell, or threaten. You don't have to screw up your courage, take a deep breath, bring along a friend. You just have to ask. But that's the thing. You *have* to ask. A cornucopia of freebies is available for the asking *that are not advertised*. So if you *don't* ask, it's like walking down the street, falling into a pile of money, dusting yourself off, and walking on. It's there for the taking.

There're enough tips in any few pages to reimburse you many times over for buying the book. Easy Asks—no energy, no stress.

Yours for the Asking

Salespeople have a lot of leeway—a lot more than they used to, a lot more than we think, a lot more than they want us to know. Here're some examples of what they can do for us if we ask.

Department stores send coupons to active users of the store's credit card but not to the rest of us. Customer Service, however, will give you the same coupons if you ask. They'll also give you coupons if you've forgotten your newspaper coupons. Sometimes you don't even have to go to Customer Service. An obliging salesperson can give you the discount right on the spot. Ask.

The linen chains also distribute coupons by mail and in newspapers, the most popular, a $5-off coupon on a minimum $15 purchase. Often as not, I leave my coupon at home. "Darn," I say.

"No problem," the clerk says, and whips out a coupon for me.

They're even casual about the $15 minimum, allowing a $13 sale to qualify. In effect, they're offering a permanent $5 discount. Come and get it.

Linen 'N Things accepts coupons from other stores. I pile them up and every few months, do a big shop. Coupons come in all forms: $5 off a $15 purchase, 30, 25, 20 percent off a single item, sometimes a single *clearance* item. One time I used eight coupons. Many were expired, but no one cared. I bought $72.91 worth of merchandise for $52.41—a savings of 28 percent.

Many stores, especially multibranch stores, will meet a lower price. I saw an ad for 20 percent off Birkenstocks, but the store was forty minutes away. Well, maybe they'd be on sale at Nordstrom, which was three minutes away.

The shoes were *not* on sale. I asked the saleswoman to match the sale price, but she wouldn't do it without seeing the ad. Since I hadn't brought the ad with me, I went to a bookstore and bought another paper.

The saleswoman then called the smaller store to determine if the particular model I wanted was on sale. (Nordstrom is really getting tough, but once the woman determined the style I wanted was included in the sale, she gave me the discount and reimbursed me for the newspaper, too.)

Most stores will give you the lower price if you have proof. Bring an ad or a number for them to call. They'll also accept another store's discount coupons—but you have to Ask. The style of briefs I like were on sale at Macy's, but there were none in my size. Robinsons-May, a few steps away, had them in stock, but no sale. They agreed to call Macy's and verify the sale price; in fact, they had a whole routine for doing so. The process took less than five minutes and saved me 40 percent.

As you can see, things are pretty flexible. That's why, if you've missed a sale, don't accept statements like, "The sale was over yesterday." There's no reason you can't get the sale price today. None at all. Ask. First ask nicely. "I wonder if you can give me the sales price?" If the salesperson resists, speak with the department manager.

For their end-of-season merchandise dump, department stores run 50- to 75-percent-off sales with an additional 20-percent-off coupon, 33 percent off just for today. . . . There are so many permutations of discounts—50 percent off the ticketed price, 50 percent off the original price, 33 percent off. Clothes are jumbled on racks, and prices are difficult to determine. If I like something, I have it scanned—especially if the ticketed price is more than I want to spend. The actual price is never what you think it will be. Usually less. Sometimes, far less. I've gotten $75 jeans for $11, a $40 knit top for $7, etc., etc. In fact, price tags don't mean a thing.

It's about as easy to get my husband into a department store as it is to get a pig to fly. (The pig, at least, is polite about it.) What this adds up to, if I want my husband to get new clothes, the easiest thing is to buy them for him. When he needed a new jacket, I saw two that I liked, so, exceptional wife that I am, I bought both of them to let him choose. And guess what? He liked both of them. That turned into a pretty hefty purchase, but I was pleased he was pleased.

The jackets had been on some sort of promotion—there's always some sort of promotion. The heavier one with the zip-out lining was reduced from a ticket price of $130 to $89.99; the lighter one went from $95 to $69.99. I also bought him a shirt which originally was $29 and now $19.99, the three items totaling $193.92.

Two weeks later, the store ran 20-percent-off coupons in the paper. Should I take the time to bring these items back and see if

I could get the discount? The store was on my way to the dentist. It would only take an extra ten minutes or so, I reasoned. I had kept the labels against such an occurrence, so I packed the jackets up in a shopping bag, having to remove one from my surprised husband's back, and headed for Robinsons-May. The shirt had already been washed, the tags tossed—you can't win them all. (No, you're right. I don't believe *that* for a minute.)

Luckily, I was helped by an obliging salesperson. "Why, we'll return the ones you bought and sell you them again using the coupon," she said.

"Darn," I said, "I should have brought the shirt."

"No problem," she said. "I can use the sales slip."

I received the discount on one of the jackets and the shirt, but the lighter-weight jacket had gone on an additional sale, and it's price had dropped even more. You'd have no idea, unless you had the items scanned. The signs were ambiguous or downright wrong. The jacket went from $69.99 to $39.99.

So if I had bought them at the full, ticketed price (and there may have been no way of doing that) I would have paid $255. With the first sale, I paid 193.92. When I brought them back with a coupon, the price dropped to $137.89, a savings of 55 percent. And it was a snap. That's why I say, price tags mean nothing.

I believe I have, on occasion, paid the ticketed price for something. I earnestly believe this, although I can't recall any specific instance.

Many stores will give you 10 percent off for opening a store charge. On large purchases, it's worth taking the five minutes to fill in the application. Among those who have offered this discount are Macy's, Bloomingdale's, Robinsons-May, Pier 1, Eddie Bauer. As of this printing, Sears does not. Nordstrom does not.

If you're married, you can open three accounts: his, hers, and ours.

You can bargain with major chains on appliances. If you can't get them to drop the price, you might get them to throw in an extended warranty.

Warning: *Something new and annoying.* The "presale." Here's how it works: In order to get a sale price, you must purchase an item today but can't take it home till the sale starts—days later. Obviously, this is a strategy to get you into the store twice. But who has the time? I endured this drill once, bought a bathrobe—actually the last one in my size. When I went to pick it up, the salesperson couldn't find it. I had to go to the Management Office for help. Eventually, they found the robe and gave it to me for free, but it wasn't worth the hassle. So I don't participate in presales anymore. I tell the salesperson the bathrobe story and Ask them to sell me the thing right then and there—at the discounted price.

Feel free to use my story.

A minimum purchase is required on cosmetic "bonus" offers, which is invariably $2 or $3 more than the lowest-priced cosmetic, thereby forcing you to buy *two* products. After being annoyed by this policy for years, I decided to Ask.

"Can you give me the bonus even though I'm under the minimum?"

"No problem," the saleswoman said and gave me the gift for less than the minimum purchase requirement. Another easy Ask.

Not all stores will do this, so find one that will. Don't be a doormat for manipulative rip-offs.

By the way, I'm starting a twelve-step program for women addicted to free cosmetic offers—WAFCOA it's called—Women Addicted to Free Cosmetic Offers Anonymous. *(If you'd like to have enough money to purchase such incidentals as food and shelter, if you're embarrassed by the overwhelming number of cutesy plastic cosmetic cases in your closet and useless cosmetic samples, come join us, use our phone list.)*

SO:

- Salespeople have a lot of discretion.
- Don't be intimidated by the "rules." If you don't have a discount coupon, you can pick one up at customer service, or simply ask the salesperson to give you the discount anyway. "Policies" are broken left and right by salespeople. Ask.
- Stores will meet sale prices at other stores. Bring the ad or get them to call the other store.
- If you like something, but it's more than you want to spend, have it scanned. Especially during sales, the ticket may not reflect the true price.
- Avoid the "presale."
- For large purchases, open a store charge account—it's usually good for 10 percent off the first purchase or the first day.
- Don't be a doormat for manipulative ripoffs.

Timing Is Everything

Discounts hide in unexpected places. Stores sometimes offer lower prices at special times to special groups. Usually, these discounts are not advertised. They're easy asks, but you have to be alert for them—and ask.

Moto Photo, for instance, gives a free second set of prints on Wednesdays and Saturdays.

Border's Books offers a 10-percent senior discount on Tuesdays.

Starbucks gives you a free "tall"—Starbonics for medium—cup of coffee for every pound of coffee beans you purchase, but you have to ask.

The UCSD (University of California, San Diego) bookstore gives a 10-percent discount on Wednesday afternoons between 4:00 and 6:00. How do I know? I just happened to be buying books at 5:00 on a Wednesday and noticed they were discounted. "How come?" I asked the clerk. "That's the policy," he answered. Nowhere did I see a sign advertising this fact. Now when I'm in a new store I try to remember to ask if they offer any special discounts.

• • •

I knew I'd missed out on a good thing when the checkout clerk at Ralphs said to the woman on line ahead of me, "We don't accept expired coupons anymore." I'd never even *tried* to use an expired coupon in a supermarket. Long ago I'd been well schooled against such a practice by A & P clerks who pounced triumphantly on expired coupons.

"This here's expired," they'd gloat.

They'd squint their myopic eyes at the fine print on the lookout for the well-known crime of coupon fraud.

"I ain't never seed one like this," they'd mutter. They must have thought I had a printing press in my basement to gin out these things. So I'd never thought to try an expired coupon at Ralphs. But you know what? I *will* try now, even though it's not their "policy." A different clerk, a different "policy." A different *day,* a different policy.

Buy off-season and save—like air conditioners. Buy them in winter. Ask for a lower price.

SO:

* Discounts hide in unusual places. Ask every merchant, "Do you offer a discount?" Or, "Are there any discounts I should know about?"
* Assumptions can trip us up. Don't assume a store won't accept an expired coupon—or another store's coupon. Ask.

Discount, Sr.

Seniors, a group identified by businesses in a variety of ways—AARP members, anyone over fifty, fifty-five, sixty-two, or sixty-five—can help themselves to a grab bag full of discounts. In addition to discounts at the movies, many department stores and fast-food chains offer senior discounts.

Ross's gives a 10-percent discount for people over fifty-five on Tuesdays.

Subway has a 10-percent senior discount. McDonald's has a senior coffee—twenty-seven cents for the sixty-four-cent size; so does Burger King. (How do I know? Don't ask. It's those biannual Big Whopper attacks, those monthly bacon-egg-and-cheese biscuit blues.)

In Southern California, Rubio's *posts* a 15-percent senior discount. Carl's Jr., Koo Koo Roo, and Pick-Up-Stix give a 10-percent discount to seniors but don't post it. Train yourself to Ask. Banana Republic, *for God's sake,* gives a 10-percent senior discount. (We found *that* out because a nice salesperson hesitantly offered it to us. No signs anywhere in the store. I was surprised they even encouraged seniors to shop there.)

My friend Harriett recently got two kittens. They were her first pets, hence her first experience with a vet. She asked and learned that her vet gives a 20-percent *senior* discount. And it's not the age of the pet, but the age of the owner. That's a hefty amount considering few people get health insurance for pets. Also, vets give discounts for multiple pets, three or more. None of this is posted. You have to Ask.

It would be great if businesses *did* post their discounts. Less embarrassing for everyone. It's tricky finding out about senior discounts. Salespeople are hesitant to offer for fear of offending, and we feel decrepit asking for them. I have to force myself to ask, "Do you have a senior discount?" Usually, if they have one, they just say yes and give it to you. No discussion of how old you are.

SO:

* No matter the establishment, be it a restaurant, clothing store, book store, ask for a discount.

Nights Inn

It's easy to get a discount on a hotel room. You don't have to accept the posted or, "rack" rate. Even in peak season, hotels will discount the rate when asked. An AAA membership is usually good for a quick 10 percent off. So is being a member of AARP. (Rarely do they ask to see the actual membership card.) By not asking for a lower rate, you're in effect, paying *more* than you should. You're passing up that pile of money in the street.

The Comfort Inn chain offers a 30-percent discount to AARP members, but *only* when you reserve through the 800 number. Calling the actual facility or pulling up at the front door will net you 10 percent off. (Yes, I found this out the hard way.) You're better off calling the 800 number from your cell phone. I've even called from a gas station across the street.

And if you're traveling off-season, there's a lot more flexibility in rates, especially toward evening. I ask for the rate and then say, "It's really late. Could you give it to us for less?"

If they think they can't "sell" the room, they might give you a *really* low rate.

On one off-season trip, we stopped at an inn in Santa Barbara. It was late and I didn't have much asking energy. Just a little.

"What's your best rate?" I asked.

"We can give you a corporate rate of $105 on a room that's usually $195. It has a view of the mountains."

"We'll take it," I said. (I'd never even asked for a *corporate* rate. What corporation? I'm self-employed, my husband's a professor.)

But the next day I overheard the receptionist quoting a rate of $79 to another couple. When they finished, I went over to her.

"I heard you quoting that couple $79 for a room. You told us your best rate was $105."

"They have a coupon."

"What kind of coupon?"

"Eh . . . Something we send out from time to time." There was a silence and finally she blurted out, "Look, okay, we'll charge you $89—$10 extra for the view."

Something similar happened at a Holiday Inn Express outside Savannah, Georgia. I first asked for the senior discount, the AAA discount, and then asked if there was any cheaper rate. The clerk looked up shyly. "If you have a coupon," she said.

"A coupon?"

"From the Shoney's ad book. There's a Shoney's across the street. You can pick up the booklet in the entrance."

Our rate went from $68 to $54 just for crossing the street. The Traveler Discount Guide distributed at Shoney's, is one of a number of "exit" discount books available at locations near freeway exits, like fast-food places, free-standing kiosks, and inexpensive restaurants. This guide is also available by calling 1-800-332-3948 or going to *www.roomsaver.com* for on-line coupons good in thirty-eight states. The booklets are chock-abloc with coupon goodies for moderate-priced facilities like Hampton Inn, Days Inn, and Holiday Inn. They're geared to same-day, "walk-in" travelers—those who don't have advance reservations. Hotels offer these discounts off-season. The Traveler Coupon Guide is another source of discount coupons for California, Nevada, and Arizona. They're at *www.exitinfo.com*, *www.coupontraveler.com*, or 1-619-401-8220. These are just examples of discounts you can stumble across if you stay alert.

SO:

- ✦ It's a snap to get a discount on a hotel room. Ask for the lowest rate.
- ✦ Stay alert—listen for deals.
- ✦ *Ask* for deals.

It's Good to Have Friends in Low Places

Harriett was wandering through Nordstrom when she noticed that a pair of pants she'd recently bought were on sale.

"Damn," she mumbled to herself, "they're on sale." A saleswoman overheard her.

"I can refund you the difference," the woman said.

"But I don't have my receipt," Harriett said.

"That's all right. You don't need a receipt."

"Well . . . ," Harriett thought for a minute. What she was about to say was true, but seemed kind of nervy. "I actually bought *two* pair." (You see why Harriett's my friend?)

"No problem," the woman said. She printed out a receipt, opened her cash drawer, and handed Harriett $67.

This was an astonishing story. Every time I thought about it, I shook my head and chuckled. The next time I was in Nordstrom, I asked a friendly saleswoman about Nordstrom's policies.

"We're trained to do whatever it takes to make the customer happy," she said. Another reminder that salespeople have a lot more discretion than we think.

And although I've never run into a salesperson waiting to hand me a stack of cash, most department stores will give you the sale price within a certain number of days, usually thirty. (Nordstrom used to refund the difference at anytime, but they've gotten tougher. They'll *do* it, but they give you a hard time. And they probably aren't taking back tires anymore either.)*

So I'll buy something I love at full price even if it's more than I want to spend, because it will probably go on sale within the month. I save my receipts and don't remove the tags. Unlike Harriett, I'm just a mere mortal.

SO:

- Stores will refund you the difference between what you paid and the new sale price within a certain period of time—usually thirty days. Keep your receipts. Don't remove tags. When an item goes on sale, ask to be refunded the difference. Then, if a store won't give you the difference, you can return the item and repurchase it at the sale price.
- Salespeople have a lot more discretion than we imagine.

*There's a story, probably mythical, that Nordstrom took back a set of tires even though they don't *carry* tires.

Discounts for Some

I realize the purpose of coupons is to get you into the store or to get you to buy a particular product, but we coupon savers are not the ones the stores are making the big bucks on. We're always looking for a deal. What would be wrong with simply advertising the discount price and giving it to everyone, instead of forcing you to save coupons?

Discounts probably aren't going to the people who really need them—those who are too sick and out-of-it to worry about coupons. A new pharmacy—part of a chain—offered $10-off coupons on new prescriptions. My copay is $20, so $10 off is a big savings—and, of course, every one of my prescriptions was new to them. So month after month, I grabbed a sale flier and ripped out the $10 coupon while the pharmacist hunted for my medication. (Ever notice how when they're flipping through the envelopes, they're shaking their heads as if no such prescription exists? "What was your name again?" they ask, shaking their heads. . . .)

This went on for a year, until one time I searched through the sale flier and there was no coupon. "Am I missing the coupon?" I asked the pharmacist.

"No, we're not giving them out anymore. It's been a year."
The prescription would now cost $20.

"Well then, don't bother," I said. "I still have some samples the doctor gave me." I started to walk away.

"Just a minute," the pharmacist said. He reached down under the counter and pulled up a $10 coupon. "This one's good till December," he said.

Amazing right? He knew about it all along, but played dumb until it became evident he was going to lose a sale.

SO:

- New pharmacies give discounts to get clients. It's easy to miss the ad or the flier, so Ask.
- Be persistent. If you can't find a coupon, Ask for one.

5.

Getting Over Your Shame of Returns, or, Many Happy Returns

W

e've paid our hard-earned money for something that turns out to be useless, defective, or even destructive, yet we hesitate to march down to the merchant and ask for a refund. Why are we reluctant to return a product or a service that doesn't satisfy? Because we confuse behavior appropriate in personal relationships with behavior appropriate in commercial situations. Even though we know we've been treated unfairly, we're reluctant to apply the same standards of behavior to business that they use on us. Actually, we're treating *ourselves* unfairly if we allow business to intimidate and manipulate us while we continue to apply the standards of "polite" society to them. The relationship between us and business is totally asymmetrical, David and Goliath.

Our confusion about how to interface with business is reflected in a *New York Times Magazine* column, "The Ethicist." In a letter to the columnist, Randy Cohen, a reader raises questions about ethical behavior and business. It seems that Microsoft was offering a $400 rebate on a computer if you signed up for Microsoft's on-line service. Evidently California law requires an open-ended cancellation policy and many people signed up for the service, got their rebate, then canceled. The reader wants to know if this was unethical behavior. The answer Cohen gives is that it is unethical only if you signed up then canceled solely to get the rebate.

Yet when Cohen reflects on how Bill Gates would behave if the shoe were on the other foot, he says, "I reach this conclusion reluctantly, because if the tables were turned and you offered a $400 rebate to Bill Gates, there's every reason to believe he would take it, and your car, and your house, and your immortal soul. At least that's the impression you form from the government's investigation of Microsoft's business practices."[1]

So what's it to be? Business can treat us unethically, but *we* have to be "good" little boys and girls?

The Ethicist is an interesting column because it inadvertently draws attention to the disparity between ethics used with individuals and ethics used by business. The columnist, Randy Cohen, takes a traditional moral attitude; but by belying it with his jokey manner, he shows his uncertainty about whether personal standards should be used in a business climate.

Part of the problem is that we feel standing up for our rights means we have to get angry, yell, stomp, and bluster. Yet we can remain calm and polite and still address our rights.

If we look at an instance where the lines between interpersonal relationships and business intersect, we can get a better understanding of the issues. On a stay at a bed-and-breakfast in Folkston, Georgia, we received hospitality way beyond the norm, especially considering the owners had just returned from the man's mother's funeral. When we went to pay the bill, I noticed that the promised 10-percent AAA discount was missing, but I decided that I would let it go. I was sure it was not a deliberate omission but rather due to the owners' stress. A business situation had turned into a personal situation, and I made a conscious choice not to change it back. The opposite happened a few days later. The promised discount was missing on the bill at another bed-and-breakfast; but here, we'd been treated like customers, not guests, so I reminded the owner of the discount.

In the first instance, I applied behaviors appropriate in inter-personal relationships; in the second, I applied business stan-dards. As an informed consumer, you get to decide when to apply *what* standards to whom.

Returning Goods

We all have different priorities. My friends span the spectrum. At one end is Harriett, who's as good at return shopping as she is at buying. Down at the other end are Lucy and Sharon, who don't even notice that they're being ripped off. When they rented a vacation car, they reported their surprise at the final cost of the car. (More about car rentals later.)

"It was a lot more than we expected," they said. And that's where the story ended. It never occurred to them to ask why!

It also never occurred to Lucy that she could return a set of flatware with a pointy shape that kept getting stuck in the dishwasher basket.

"If you're not satisfied with it, why don't you take it back?" I suggested.

"Oh," Lucy said. "I never *thought* of that."

But that was long ago. Today, Lucy and Sharon credit me with raising their awareness *and* their nerve.

Somewhere else on the spectrum is my friend "Ellen," who's proud of returning an electric blanket to a large department store. She was satisfied with the blanket until she read about the possible dangers of electromagnetic radiation. She took the blanket back and told the store about the article. They gave her a refund. This is an example of a simple, appropriate action that resulted in a prompt, satisfactory response. Most people would be glad to have such a harmonious transaction. (By the way, don't go throwing out your electric blanket, those findings have since been disputed.)

SO:

- If you have a problem with something you bought, or a service you contracted for, you have a right to ask for a satisfactory explanation.
- Return and expect a full refund for anything that might be hazardous.
- We all have different priorities. You get to decide what's important to you, throwing something in the garbage or bringing it back. But if you decide to do nothing, don't make your decision out of fear or thinking you don't have rights. We have the right to ask for anything.

Sweat the Small Stuff

What else would I do for fun?

If it doesn't satisfy, take it back. The wart remover doesn't work, the antifungal doesn't perform, take them back. If you've kept the receipt, most stores don't even ask why. If you haven't, they'll usually let you pick up comparably priced items.

At the supermarket, *anything* can be returned. *You* have to decide what's worth the effort. Aside from the obvious—overripe fish or slightly off meat—I've returned such things as disappointing melons and never-to-ripen pineapples. You can return without receipts, though some specialty chains will give you a little grief.

As for clothes, they should last for more than one season, or, **Let No Garment Pill Before Its Time.** I keep receipts for at least two years. Clothes that are treated normally, that is washed according to manufacturer's directions and worn a reasonable number of times should last more than one season. They shouldn't shrink, fade, ball, or stretch. If they do, they go back.

It's no news that in today's marketplace you can return any *un*used item to the store where it was purchased with, and sometimes without, a receipt. The *news* is that you can also return these items to stores where they *weren't* bought. Business mergers have actually made returns easier. Federated Department Stores, for instance, owns Macy's, but it also owns Bloomingdales. (And Burdines, Rich's, Stern's, Lazarus, Fingerhut, Goldsmith's, the Bon Marché.) You can generally return something to any of the stores for full credit. If they don't carry it, they can find it in the computer. If it was a gift and you therefore don't have a receipt, they'll give you store credit. The May Department Stores Company owns Lord &Taylor, Hecht's, Strawbridge's, Foley's, Robinsons-May, Filene's, Kaufmann's, Famous-Barr, L.S. Ayres, the jones store, Meier & Frank, ZCMI.

And now for that department where we spend a great deal of time and money—the Cosmetics Department. Talk about manipulation! The cosmetics industry has us believing that what we look like in the morning is unacceptable, that in addition to washing our faces, we must moisturize, exfoliate, tone, coverup, powder, mask, conceal, hydrate, purify—have I missed anything? We're intimidated and shamed by cosmetic saleswomen into buying outrageously priced products that actually don't make us young, beautiful, or thin.

After this buildup, you can bet I return cosmetics that disappoint. Cosmetics are a snap to return to department stores or drug stores. In fact, you can return "designer" cosmetics to any department store—for a full refund. You don't even have to return it to the place you purchased it. You don't even need a receipt.

Another thing that sends me rushing back to cosmetic counters is a design "defect" in the packaging. Two-thirds of the way into a tube of facial cleanser, and the rest won't budge. I suppose *we're* designed to chuck it at that point. That's what I *used* to do. Now I bring it back for a refund or a replacement.

You can even return things to businesses that post a NO RETURNS policy. I thought I was stuck and wouldn't be able to return a set of mugs to the Pier 1 Clearance Store. At home, I realized they weren't microwave proof and, therefore, of limited use. I like to microwave my tea, and you got a good scalding with these mugs. Assuming—there it is that word—assuming because I'd bought the mugs at the Clearance Store, they wouldn't be returnable, I'd thrown out the receipt. Well, I was stuck. Forty dollars down the drain.

The next time I was at the Clearance Store, I noticed the return policy printed at the bottom of the receipt. NO REFUNDS it proclaimed boldly. But the small print said, "Merchandise exchanges only . . . accompanied by this receipt." And I'd chucked the receipt. Still, it wouldn't hurt to ask.

Without much hope and in a negatively framed question, I said to the checkout clerk. "I bought some mugs that I'm really disappointed with, but I threw away the receipt. I suppose you couldn't—"

"No problem. Bring them in. We'll be glad to give you store credit." Just like that. More accommodating than I would ever have imagined.

When I was getting ready to move cross-country, I mentioned to a supermarket clerk that I wished I didn't have so many canned goods to pack—movers charge by the pound (roughly sixty-five cents).

"Oh, you don't have to take them with you," she said. "We'd

be happy to give you a full refund." So I brought in those extra pounds of ugly fat—and left with $20 in my pocket.

Sometimes, they ask you. I'd gotten an Orrefors vase as a gift, which didn't do much for me. Where it was purchased was nowhere discoverable. Probably a regift. I'd have to stick it in a closet and regift it also.

Then one day while I was walking through Nordstrom, I noticed the same vase in the gift department. A saleswoman watched as I stopped and examined it. "Would you like to buy it?" she asked.

No, I told her, I'd been given the same vase and wasn't crazy about it, but I didn't know where it had been bought.

"If it's in its original box with the label," she said, "*we'll* take it back."

An unwanted gift brought a $50 refund.

SO:

- You can return *anything*—tasteless melons, over-the-counter drugs, cosmetics, clothes that have not worn well.
- *You* get to decide what's worth the trouble of returning.
- Supermarkets will take back anything.
- Purchases made at one store can be returned to another store under the same corporate umbrella.
- Ask even if signs and receipts proclaim NO RETURNS. Rules are often bent just for the asking.
- Stores may exchange something you haven't even bought from them if they carry the same item.
- Once again, salespeople have a lot of discretion.

Painless Return

Here's an easy return I didn't even think of, though I always feel uncomfortable when the dental hygienist tries to sell me the latest supersonic gizmo. It seems somehow inappropriate for them to be hawking stuff at the dentist. And intimidating. If you don't buy this product, the message seems to be, your teeth will fall out. And every time you go, it's a *different* thingy they're pushing. My friend Juliet ended up with an electric brush she was unhappy with—but not for long.

She E-mailed me her story.

Mon, 17 Jul 2000 16:53:10 -0700

Dear Barbara,

I just got back from the dentist and I was CHEERFUL, in spite of the fact that the root canal he performed revealed an infection and an abscess. Why am I cheerful? I successfully returned the electric toothbrush his hygienist sold me last month, claiming that it would take off much more plaque. In fact, it did a worse job than a manual toothbrush and is outrageously expensive due to the fact that it is available only in dental offices. He took it back without a word. Before I met you I would never have even thought of returning it. You have really given me a new perspective on buying and returning.

While we're at the dentist, a close friend of mine who will remain nameless (and toothless) recently was fitted for dentures. At her next cleaning, she asked the dentist for a discount since there were only nine teeth left to clean. After he dropped *his* teeth, he agreed to prorate the cleaning.

SO:

- You don't have to be stuck with a useless product.
- Health-care professionals, such as dentists and dermatologists, often sell products that may or may not be helpful to you. Be discriminating; it's okay to try the product, but don't hesitate to ask for a refund if it's not for you. The health-care worker may have confused your best interests with a business bottom line.
- Discounts are available in all sorts of places. If you stay alert, you may discover unusual ones.

Damaged Goods

We bought an "easy to assemble" computer desk at Office Depot. ("Easy to assemble" might be the three most dreaded words in the English language.) After lugging the thing up three flights of stairs and partially assembling it, we noticed a small chip in the veneer. There was no way, at this point, we could return the desk. I called the store and asked the manager for a discount. He offered to take off 10 percent, I asked for 20. He agreed, but I would have to bring in my receipt. That meant time. To make it worthwhile, I checked the current week's ads to see if anything we'd bought last week had gone on sale. Sure enough, the office chair was $20 off. The half hour it took to accomplish the return netted me $50.

SO:

- Ask for a discount on damaged merchandise.
- Counteroffer their first offer.
- If you're returning to a store soon after you made a purchase, check to see if your purchase is now on sale—at that store, or any other.

The Law of Returns

This story is about challenging the tyrannical trio of tradition, habit, and custom to get what we need, want, and deserve—in this case, a refund on a prescription drug, something most of us would never dream of asking for. Yet our assumption—that it's out of the question to return prescription drugs—doesn't make much sense. Everything else is returnable at pharmacies and stores containing pharmacies. Why not return a prescription drug that hasn't lived up to its promise?

I'm not the world's worst sleeper, but a little help is always a good thing. My doctor prescribed a new sleeping pill touted to provide six solid hours of sleep. Because this was a nongeneric drug, it was expensive. I had a full copay of $20.

The pill quickly induced a blissful sleep—*for an hour and a half!* Then I was up and ready to make my insomnia work for me—call airlines, empty the dishwasher, pay bills. The same thing happened the next night. This drug was a dud, for me anyway. I'd wasted $20 on the little capsules.

Or had I? Why couldn't I return them the same way I'd return a nonprescription drug that didn't work? I ran this idea past my husband and friend Harriett, who both decided to vacate for another planet while I did *this* return. This assumption of the nonreturnability of prescriptions had made it deep into the consciousness of even these unflappable returners.

In fact, it took a few days to work myself into the right state.

"I have a problem," I said to the young woman at the pharmacy counter when I'd finally gotten myself over there. "This drug is supposed to give six hours of sleep, but it only worked for an hour and a half."

"That's too bad," she said. "I was going to try it myself, but you need to ask your doctor . . ."

"I'll do that," I said, "but my copay was $20 and I'd like to get that back."

The young woman looked shocked. "We can't do that," she said. "Once a prescription is opened, we can't take it back. We couldn't use it again."

"If this were an over-the-counter medication, you could take it back," I said.

"Then we could return it to the manufacturer."

"That's what I want you to do here."

"We can't, it's against the law."

"What law?" I asked.

"You'll have to talk with the manager," she said.

So later that day I called the store and asked to speak with the head of the Pharmacy Department for the entire chain. He was courteous and said he'd "make an exception in my case, just this time," and refund the $20. I thanked him and pressed on.

"I'm trying to understand," I said, "why you'll take back any other item in the store, no questions asked—without a receipt—but *not* prescription medications."

"It's against the law," he said. (That "law" again.) "We can't take the medication back and resell it. Once it's out of our hands, it could be tampered with. We would have to destroy it, and it's not just a matter of flushing it down the toilet. It's considered hazardous waste. . . ."

I interrupted him. "You wouldn't reuse an over-the-counter sleep medication, would you?"

"No."

"Would you get reimbursed by the manufacturer?"

"No, we'd just absorb the expense . . . which *could* get passed on to the consumer," he threatened.

"So in both cases, over-the-counter and prescription, you don't get reimbursed by the manufacturer?"

"That's right," he said. "But with prescription drugs, there are so many side effects, they often don't work the way they're supposed to—there are medication failures all the time and they're so expensive. We'd take a bath if we took them back. We wouldn't be in business for long."

"So it's a business decision?"

"Yes, it's a business decision."

So much for "the law."

When I talked with a pharmacist friend, he told me that the "law" only says you can't *reuse* drugs. It doesn't say they can't be returned. Typically, he said, a store's return policy—posted near the Customer Service desk—says you can return *any* merchandise. There are no disclaimers. But employees are instructed to dissuade people from returning prescription drugs, and the most effective way to do that is by invoking the sacred words, "the law."

This story is also about being too intimidated to apply methods to businesses that they use on us. The sacred invoking of "the law" is a cold-blooded tactic to get us to behave in ways that are profitable to business. And drug companies want it both ways. They want to freely advertise their medications in magazines and on TV—so that we'll nag our docs into prescribing them—

but they don't want us to return these products when they don't work. If they can manipulate us with advertising—do *you* read the fine print in the ads for the miracle drugs?—they should have liberal return policies.

This incident is also about not taking no for an answer, of pushing on, and not being intimidated by phrases like "the law." And it's an example of breaking out of the box. Tradition, habit, custom tells us we *don't* return prescription drugs. We might ask ourselves what else does this trio of tradition, habit, and custom prevent us from doing?

According to my pharmacist friend, by the way, I didn't break new ground. (Darn.)

"You wouldn't believe what people try to return," he said. "A relative dies and they bring in their leftover drugs. 'We don't need these anymore, and we'd like a refund.' Then there are those who take an antibiotic for nine days and don't feel any better—they probably shouldn't be taking it in the first place, but doctors get pressured into prescribing. So this person wants a refund for the *full* prescription because he doesn't feel better."

SO:

* Question tradition, habit, custom.
* Keep asking questions till you get an answer you like.
* If the clerk can't or won't help you, go to the next level of command.
* Don't be intimidated by words like "the law" or "company policy."
* Prescription drugs are like any other product—they're sold for profit, and you have the right to be satisfied with their effectiveness for you.

Dirty Dishes Come Clean

I expected this next return to be a real challenge, but it turned out to be easy.

Among the many appliances we bought for our new home was a dishwasher. On one-time purchases of large appliances or electronics, I buy name brands from reputable merchants rather than search for bargains. I'll wait for a sale, or *ask* for a discount, but I'm willing to pay more for good service. *Consumer Reports* is our buying guide, and the machine they rated highest was a Sear's Kenmore.

This dishwasher was equipped with a dirt-sensor, the latest technology. The more dirt, the more the washing time. Sounded good, so you can imagine our disappointment when the dishes didn't come out any cleaner than the ten-year-old junker had gotten them.

According to the repairman, the problem was that our dishes weren't dirty enough. Because we don't cook much, our dishes were too clean for this technology; and, as a result, whatever dirt we *did* accumulate, stayed there. My husband suggested we save Cheerio dust and pour it in, but that would mean eating a lot of Cheerios. In short, the dishwasher was a dud—for us, anyway. We needed a *less*-advanced system for our lifestyle.

What to do? I'd never heard of anyone returning a major appliance. But my husband was adamant. This dishwasher was not for us. It needed to be returned. We geared ourselves up and worked out a plan—he would do the talking—we'd ask to speak to a manager. Yadda, yadda, yadda.

Probably, none of our extensive preparations were necessary. We told the manager our problem, and she simply said, "Just pick out another one and we'll credit you the difference if it's less." That was all. No arguments, no pressure. In short, good service.

We chose one with a less-advanced technology that cost $100 less and cleans our soiled dishes beautifully. Sears credited us with the $100, picked up the old one, and delivered the new one with no charge to us.

SO:

+ It's worth paying more for reliability.
+ You don't have to "live" with an unsatisfactory product.
+ Ask even when you think there's no chance of a positive answer.
+ You can even return major appliances.

Come Again?

A 900-mhz phone-answering machine I'd bought at Office Depot was inadequate from the git-go. It audibly channel-searched, the messages on the answering machine were *in*audible, yet I let more than thirty days go by before doing anything about it. *Nine* months after I purchased it, I called the store and asked if I could return the phone. The salesman cited the thirty-day refund policy. There was nothing he could do.

I'd have to eat this purchase, I concluded. I'd waited too long. But it eckled me. A few weeks later I called and spoke with the manager, which I should have done in the first place. In my nicest voice, I wondered if he could "help me." I mentioned that as I had a home office, I bought a lot at Office Depot. He said he'd give me store credit for $120 on the $150 phone, which seemed fair to me considering I'd used it for nine months.

Technology had, of course, improved, and I was able to replace the phone with a much better one for an extra $10. All because I'd asked. "Store policy," was swept aside, and I was easily accommodated.

SO:

- ✦ Ask for help, don't complain.
- ✦ If you're not getting help at one level, bump up to the next level.
- ✦ If you're a frequent customer at the store, mention that. They want to keep you satisfied.
- ✦ "Store policy" is for those who don't ask.

Beware of Unadvertised Store Policies

Returning electronic equipment has become tricker thanks to a new trend in retailing. Some computer stores now charge "restocking" fees for returned computers in open boxes—even those returned within the thirty-day period. My young friend Jason found out about the fee the hard way when he tried to return a computer that was too noisy. He was assessed a 15-percent restocking fee—a shock because he hadn't been informed of the policy when he purchased the computer.

He got nowhere with on-site management, so he took his problem to the next level and E-mailed the corporate offices.

Letter to CompUSA Customer Service:
30 October 1999

I recently had a very poor shopping experience at your CompUSA store in Maryland. On September 4, 1999, I purchased a computer. After a few days of using the PC, I was not satisfied with its performance. I spoke to a tech support person who said that I could return the PC for a full refund. Once I got to the store, though, I was told I would incur a 15 percent restocking fee. The sales clerk at the Customer Service desk said that the restocking fee is applied to all opened products. I protested that a tech support person at the store told me something different about the return policy. When I could not remember the name of the person I spoke with, I was told I would have to pay the 15 percent restocking fee if I wished to return the product.

At this point, I asked to see the Store Manager and he also insisted I pay the 15 percent restocking fee if I wanted a full return. Alternatively, the Store Manager did allow me to exchange the PC for another PC at CompUSA for no additional fee. Once again, I was not pleased with its performance. I finally decided to "pay" the 15 percent restocking fee and put the entire episode behind me.

In the past, I have always had exceptional service at CompUSA, but I am so bitter about this experience that I will most likely not shop at CompUSA in the future.

I would like a store credit or full refund for the restocking fee of $248.82. If you decide to refund this money to me, I will change my disheartened opinion about CompUSA.

Thank You,

Jason K

Jason's persistence worked. (He's Harriett's son, by the way, so it's no surprise.) He E-mailed me the results.

Hi Barbara: A mostly frustrating tale with a happy ending. I E-mailed this complaint on October 30; by November 10 a CompUSA clerk credited the restocking fee to my Visa account.

SO:

- You can contest any practice that you have not been informed of.
- Don't be a doormat for manipulative sales ripoffs. Stand up for your rights. Be persistent.
- If you can't get help at one level, go to the next—in this case, Customer Service through the Internet.
- Never accept strange-sounding charges. A "restocking fee" should be the *retailer's* cost of doing business, not the customer's.

Walk in My Shoes

My husband was very attached to an expensive pair of casual dress shoes he'd had for a while. He noticed that the rubber soles were disintegrating—pieces were falling out and there was a crack across the instep.

"I'm bringing these back to Nordstrom," he said. "They shouldn't be falling apart. I haven't worn them that much."

I gulped. The shoes predated our relationship. They were *at least* five years old. Even *I* would have thrown them in the garbage.

I had to tell myself to mind my own business.

We headed off to Nordstrom. "This is your baby," I said. "I'll just hover in the background."

A determined man, he said, "That's fine."

Once in the store, he went over to a salesman. "I wonder if you can help me," he asked, and showed him the shoes.

"Would you like a new pair?" the salesman asked.

"Yes," my husband said, and we left with a new pair of $200 shoes.

SO:

- You can return *anything*.
- Ask for the outrageous.

6.
Returning Services

So far we've talked about getting refunds for unsatisfactory products. There's another category of returns besides merchandise, and that's services. We spend a significant amount of money on entertainment, recreation, and relaxation. While what we buy is not tangible, we still have the right to be satisfied with the quality of the product. We should not walk away feeling as if we'd thrown away time and money. Services are something we purchase and we can return if we have not been satisfied. We can ask for a refund, partial or whole. The same rule applies to services as it does to goods, namely, anything is returnable.

A Night at the Movies, or, That's Entertainment

At the movie *Up at the Villa,* the soundtrack went staticky, and we were unable to hear at the most critical points. After the movie, we informed the manager of the problem, and he gave us free tickets for our next movie, which seemed more than fair.

We had another bad soundtrack on a rental movie from Blockbuster. It had been an especially hectic day, and my husband and I were looking forward to plopping down and watching a good movie. No such luck. The soundtrack was completely messed up and even our desperation to watch a movie couldn't get us through it.

When I returned to Blockbuster the next day, the clerk said she'd be glad to give us another tape of the movie. But that wouldn't compensate us for not having been able to see a movie last night, I told her.

"It's random," she said. "It could happen to anyone, so the policy is just to give a replacement."

"That's not good enough," I said.

"What would you like?" she asked.

It's important to be specific about what you want, so I told her what would satisfy me. "An additional movie for free," I said.

"We can do that," she said, "but only on a favorite" (translation—old movie you've seen already).

"A recent release," I countered.

"Okay," she said.

You've finally found the movie you've been wanting to see for weeks. At home, you pop it into your VCR, only to discover it's not the movie you thought you rented. That's what happened to me—once. Now I check the jacket to make sure it contains the right movie. (Or take a chance, the movie I got was actually much better than the one I'd wanted to see.)

My daughter asks for—and receives—refunds on movies she walks out on.

SO:

* You don't have to accept the "company policy" excuse.
* You don't have to take the first offer.
* Tell the merchant the remedy you're looking for.
* Check to see if the movie you're renting is the one you meant to rent.
* Movies are a product like any other. If you're not satisfied with the movie, ask to be compensated, for a replacement, for a refund. This same policy applies to CDs and cassettes.

It's Greek to Me

Restaurant dinners fall into both the goods *and* services categories; and if we're not satisfied in either of these categories, we're entitled to be compensated. Seems logical, doesn't it? Yet when the waiter asks, "How is everything?" we nod robotically. "Fine," we say. Why do we have such trouble being truthful? It's because we confuse eating in a restaurant with eating in someone's home. Naturally, we say "fine" in someone's house—if you want to be invited back—but we need to remember that when we go to a restaurant, we're dealing with a business. We're *paying*.

In the past five years, there's been a massive increase in the frequency with which people eat at restaurants. For many of us, it's more often than not. And because of the suddenness of this phenomenon, we haven't developed social tools, a code of behavior to interact productively. We don't have to feel embarrassed to tell the waiter about any aspect of the meal that's unsatisfactory because good restaurants actually want to know if something's wrong.

At a dinner some years ago with a male friend from an old, socially prominent family, the dish I ordered, which was normally scrumptious, lacked flavor. When the waiter came by to ask about our dinner, I wasn't up to pretending.

"It's okay," I said, unconvincingly.

"Are you sure?" he asked.

"Well . . ."

"We'll be glad to take it off your bill or replace it with something else," he said.

My friend was mortified. Simply mortified. "*We* don't do that," he said, referring to the entire upper class, to which I obviously didn't belong.

Well, *we* do do that. Or can learn to. It's good for us; it's good for restaurants.

Recently, we went with some acquaintances to a favorite Greek restaurant. I ordered an expensive shrimp dish I'd been wanting to try—Shrimp à la Grêque—jumbo shrimp with linguine and feta cheese in a tomato sauce. The shrimp were awful—mushy and off-tasting. Since the people we were with were new friends, I felt inhibited about sending the dish back, and, instead, filled up on salad and bread. I even let the waiter put the leftovers in a doggie bag.

The next morning I saw the Styrofoam container in the frig and decided to take action. The restaurant was within walking distance from our house, so just before lunch, I carried the thing back. It was heavy—I'd barely made a dent. I asked to speak to the manager.

When I told him about the mushy shrimp, he shook his head in agreement. "Yes," he said, "this time of the year, the shrimp aren't any good. We can't get them from Mexico. We have to get them from Asia. I had the dish yesterday and was terribly disappointed. But you should have said something last night."

Of course he was right. "I should have," I said, "but we were with strangers, and I didn't feel comfortable."

"I understand," he said, "but we can't really correct something if you don't tell us about it. I'll be glad to refund you the price of the dish ($15.99), but the next time, please tell us about it then and there so we can make it right."

(Why they serve this dish when they couldn't get good shrimp, I have no idea. The waiter should at least issue a warning.)

Good restaurants *want* to know if a customer is dissatisfied—in this country, that is. Not true in other cultures. In France, for instance, no one comes around and asks, "How is everything?" It's assumed that everything is not only fine but superb. Last summer, in France, I sent back a lukewarm bowl of soup—and caused a furor. The waiter was mortified but also sure that I was incorrect. You could see he thought the soup was just right. No apologies, no replacement—and we were charged for the bum soup. Different countries, different customs.

Even in this country, restaurateurs "fresh off the boat" are not interested in how you like the food. It's strictly caveat emptor. We got mildly ill after eating at a Chinese restaurant that normally serves some of the best food on the planet. When I called the manager, he was uninterested, told me the usual: No one has ever . . . We were the first. . . . I didn't take the complaint any further because we really enjoy eating there, and unless I called the Board of Health, I'd get nowhere.

SO:

• If something doesn't satisfy, tell your server immediately. A good restaurant wants to know.

- Ask the waiter if the dish is good before you order it. Perhaps he will fess up to the bum shrimp. If he doesn't, you can hold him responsible.
- When the waiter comes by to ask how everything is, tell how your dish *really* is.
- Different cultures have different customs. In France, if you complain about a dish or a preparation, you might get thrown out on your ear.

A Piece of Cake

Every year on his birthday, my husband takes his graduate students to dinner. This year he picked an up-scale Italian restaurant. When I made the reservation, I mentioned that it was a birthday celebration, anticipating they'd do the whole birthday thing—a piece of cake with a candle and a serenade in Italian. Not only did they forget the birthday, but the service, in general, was poor. You had to beg for water, bread, and parmesan cheese.

I called the next day and asked to speak with the manager.

"We love your restaurant and eat there often," I said, "but last night, we were so disappointed." I went on to tell her of the forgotten birthday and the other problems.

"That's terrible," she said. Now *that's* the kind of response we all love to hear. No stone-walling, obfuscating, denial. "Who was your server?" she asked.

Gulp. I hate ratting on someone. "Actually our server was very nice; it just seemed as if everyone was very busy. It was a crowded night."

"It was crowded, but everything was under control," she said. "You shouldn't have been neglected like that." In fact, she was right. I gave her the name of the server, again stressing that he was very sweet.

"We're really sorry," she said, "and I'm going to send you a gift certificate to express our concern."

We've returned to this restaurant many times since and always have good feelings about it.

SO:

* Instead of complaining, tell the restaurant of your disappointment.
* A good restaurant will try to compensate you for a bad experience.

A Tall Fish Tale, or, Be Careful, You May Get What You Ask For

Sometimes, you may be surprised by what you get. The following is a story of how asking can have a funny outcome.

My future husband and I went to dinner at a popular fish restaurant—one that he'd been to often before we met. He'd spoken highly of it, and this was supposed to be a special treat. At the end of the meal, we looked at each other. The dinner was more than disappointing. The fish was overcooked and not especially fresh, and the prices were exorbitant.

It was at the beginning of our relationship, and we were mutually unsure of how to handle this. Finally, we blurted out in unison, "This food wasn't very good."

"We just won't come here again," David said, and we left.

If I'd been alone, I would have sent my dish back; but others, including my future husband, find this kind of thing embarrassing. They'd rather live with an unacceptable dish than allow what to them is an unpleasant note into the dinner. So if I'm having dinner with friends, I ask them if they'd mind before I send a dish back. This is another instance where behaviors appropriate with a friend can intersect with behaviors appropriate with business. It's a complex situation where there's more at stake than you versus business, and it's a good illustration of the different behaviors appropriate in each situation. Though you may feel perfectly justified in giving an honest answer when the waiter asks, "How is everything?" you might have to sacrifice getting your "just desserts" in order not to make a friend feel uncomfortable.

(By now, three years later, my husband is perfectly comfortable with my sending a dish back and even does so himself if something's really awful.)

The next day, in the privacy of my office, I called the restaurant manager and told him of our disappointment. He was apologetic and sent us a gift certificate for $40 toward another dinner.

A few weeks later, armed with our gift certificate and thoughts of a good dinner, we returned, hoping that the last time had been a fluke (or a flounder.)

We decided not to order broiled fish as we had last time, so I ordered fried oysters and my husband, steamed halibut. My oysters were fine. As to his dish, when he dug into the halibut, his fork went down a fourth of an inch then chunged into a rubbery, unyielding substance, the best use for which would be shoe leather. Our waitress noticed him pounding away at the tough flesh.

"My goodness," she said. "It's not cooked." She whisked the plate out from under him. "I'll send the manager over," she said.

We looked at each other in amused amazement. This place was too bad to be true.

The manager arrived immediately with a wringing of hands. "I wouldn't blame you if you never came back," he said.

And believe me, he's had no cause to blame us.

SO:

- + If you're not satisfied with a restaurant meal, you have every right to inform the restaurant and expect them to try to satisfy you.
- + Behaviors appropriate in personal relationships can intersect with behaviors appropriate in business relationships.

Is Everything Okay?

Hotel stays are another form of service. If we are not satisfied with any aspect of a hotel stay, we're entitled to ask for and expect reimbursement or compensation. Reputable hotels want their customers to be satisfied, and they can only know if their service is satisfactory if we let them know, yet here too, many are reluctant to do so. Like my friend Sharon. A few summers ago, she and I took a trip through Nova Scotia. We were traveling on a budget, but the last night of the trip, we decided to splurge and stay at an expensive resort, a classy château from the twenties.

I had a headache and was looking forward to relaxing in luxury; but when we checked in, we were hustled off to an unrenovated room down the hall from the reception desk. It was minuscule and dated. You had to twist your body into an unusual shape to see the TV. The door to the bathroom was partially blocked by a bureau. We were so disappointed. We should have spoken up and asked for a better room, but I had a headache and Sharon disliked what she considers confrontation. We'd make do, we decided. It was only one night. (This was a really *bad* headache.)

After we settled in, we went to sit on the terrace and read. A man who identified himself as the hotel manager came over to us and asked if we were enjoying our stay. I sighed. Between the headache and the fact that Sharon hated confrontation. . . . This was an opportunity I decided to pass up. Or try to.

"It's okay . . . ," I said.

"Is there something wrong?" he asked.

"Well . . . The room is a little disappointing."

"I'm sorry to hear that," he said. And he actually *sounded* sorry. "What room did they give you?" When we told him, he sighed with exasperation.

"The hotel's not filled," he said. "I don't know why they gave you that room."

(*Two women traveling alone,* I thought.)

"Would you allow me to change your room?" he asked.

"We've already spread out our things," I said. "And I have this headache . . ."

"Oh, I know about headaches!" he cried. "You suffer from headaches, too! They're so awful. I have to get into bed for the day. Please, let me have all of your things taken to another room. You won't have to do a thing."

"We'll take it!" Sharon jumped in.

The "room" was actually a private cabin with two bedrooms, two baths, a living room with a fireplace—the logs ready to be lit—and a basket of fruits, cheeses, and sweets. We screamed with happiness, jumped up and down, and hugged each other. For once, Sharon appreciated my speaking up.

SO:

- Don't take the first room you're offered if it's not acceptable.
- If you have an open and friendly attitude, good things fall in your lap.
- At reputable businesses, management wants to know how to satisfy you. Tell them.

A Good Night's Sleep

It's often the case that large hotel chains are more responsive to customer satisfaction than smaller establishments. If they don't meet a certain level of quality, they'll refund your money without hassle. Hampton Inns, for example, advertises a no-questions-asked refund policy if you're not totally satisfied. Holiday Inn leaves a brochure in every room that advertises the "Holiday Inn Hospitality Promise. Making your stay a complete success is our goal. Just let our Manager on Duty or front desk staff know if any part of your stay isn't satisfactory. We promise to make it right, or you won't pay for that part of your stay."[1] (Translation: They'll knock some off the price of your room if you have specific complaints.)

That's what happened to us on a recent trip to Savannah, where we stayed at a beautiful old hotel that was now owned by Holiday Inn. Everything was fine until we went to sleep. Then the air-conditioning fan, which was directly over our heads, blasted cold air into our faces. We tried to open the windows but they were sealed shut, so we called the front desk. They sent a repairman who directed the fan away from our heads. I called the manager and told her of our disappointment.

"We'll be glad to take 30 percent off the price of your room to make up for the inconvenience," she said. The room was $150 a night and we were staying for three nights.

This was all accomplished politely—no scenes, no threats—and all from the comfort of our room.

A recent, annoying trend in medium- to lower-priced facilities is the use of dim lighting. I don't think it's *only* to save energy; it's also a good concealer. (One of the major differences in hotel quality is the number of rooms per hour the housekeeping staff is required to clean; obviously, the lower the number, the better the quality.) Thanks to the dim lighting, I didn't see the swarms of ants in my room until the next morning. I told the manager of my displeasure and asked for a reduction in my rate. He said there was nothing he could do; I should have said something when I checked in: the catch-22 answer.

I saw I was getting nowhere, so I paid my bill and called the chain's Customer Service once I was home. The facility I'd stayed at was individually owned, so Customer Service contacted them first. When the manager "declined responsibility," Customer Service sent me a certificate for $40 off a future stay.

Since our trip to France was at the height of the season, it was necessary to reserve ahead. Because of the nine-hour time difference, I faxed and E-mailed requests for rooms in my fractured French. Luckily, I noticed on one of the return faxes, a Best Western imprint under the hotel's name. When I called the Best Western 800 number, I learned that Best Western was affiliated with hundreds of small hotels in Europe of a higher quality than the Best Westerns in the States. All you had to do was call the

800 number to book. No more faxes in broken French. Plus, they offered a 10-percent senior discount. Better than a kick in the pants, as my grandfather used to say. There was an equivalent 800 number in Europe, which gave us a great deal of flexibility in changing our plans en route.

For the traveler on a modest budget, these hotels are small, charming, and personally run. Rooms range from $75 to $125. "Best Western is not only the world's biggest lodging brand; all of its properties are independently owned and operated. They are gathered under the Best Western banner not as franchises but in an association whose members pay for marketing, national advertising, the toll-free reservations number and similar expenses."[2]

Another advantage of dealing with a large corporation became evident when a few weeks after we returned home, we received a bill for a room we thought we'd canceled. In a panic, I tore through our receipts. There it was—the cancellation number. I keep cancellation numbers for months against something like this happening. When I called the 800 number, they said they'd inform the hotel not to charge our credit card. You *know* we would have had a lot of hassle if this hotel hadn't been under the Best Western aegis.

Other U.S. chains have numerous facilities in Europe; and of course, there are European chains, but I don't know if their customer-service policies are as customer friendly.

S O:

- ✦ Dealing with chains and franchises assures responsiveness to customer needs.
- ✦ If you can't get help at one level, climb the ladder.
- ✦ Ask to be compensated for your inconvenience.
- ✦ Keep a file with cancellation numbers.

A Definite "No"

Air travel is another service for which the provider can be held accountable. My husband and I had to cancel a trip because I had a sinus infection and my doctor didn't think it was safe for me to fly. I asked her to write a letter stating this so we could get our tickets refunded.

When I took the tickets and the letter to a nearby American Airlines ticket office, a condescending ticket agent told me that the airline "didn't do that anymore." We'd have to pay a $75 change fee when we had new tickets issued. The supervisor sang the same song, in the same condescending manner.

Later that day I invoked my family rule: If you don't get the answer you want from "Tracey," call back later and talk to "Michele"; you might get an answer you like better. Airline policies are so complex and changeable, even employees are confused. I called the 800 number but was given the same answer. American Airlines no longer had that policy. They couldn't do anything for me, "Michele" said—and she *wasn't* condescending.

This was discouraging. Three people, one of them a supervisor, gave me the same negative answer. The door was closed.

There was no hope. In a faint voice, I asked Michele to connect me with Customer Service.

"I can't put you through to them; they don't allow that," she said. "You'll have to write a letter."

Half-heartedly, I sent off a letter. Why was I wasting my time?

March 17, 1999

Consumer Relations
American Airlines
P.O. Box 619612
MD 2400
DWF Airport, Texas 75261

Dear Sirs;

I'm writing to you for your help. Because of an illness, a sinus infection that is not responding to antibiotics and for which I will require surgery, my husband and I had to cancel a long-awaited trip to Florida to visit my parents. We were to leave tomorrow on flight #2090. (A copy of our itinerary is enclosed.)

Much to my surprise, I learned from Michele in Tucson, who was very helpful and courteous and did her best, that even with a letter from my surgeon/oncologist, we will still be levied the $75 change fee.

My husband, David, and I fly almost exclusively American. We both have Citibank AAdvantage cards and MCI WorldCom accounts. We're planning to travel to France on American this summer. We have been most pleased in our dealings with your airline.

I'm hoping that you could accommodate us by waiving the $150 that we would be penalized for canceling this trip. I'm enclosing the letter from my doctor also asking for your help.

Thank you for your assistance,
Barbara Rollin

Their answer included the following: *This letter serves as authorization to waive the administrative service fee when (your) tickets for travel to West Palm Beach on March 28, 1999, are reissued.*

Incredible. The underlings had been adamant. I was sure I was wasting my time writing a letter. The words "company policy" had been hurled at me by three airline employees, chanted like a mantra—the broken-record technique, a tactic used to discourage further inquiries. These employees may have believed what they told me, or they may not have had the authority to do more.

A friend was assessed a $50 fee by American Airlines for redepositing frequent-flier miles into her account when her travel plans changed. After hearing about my success, she wrote to American and asked to have the fee waived. Two weeks later she received a letter from American's Passenger Refunds Department telling her that "the refund you requested has been processed," and she would be credited on her next Visa statement. They thanked her "for the opportunity to be of service and for choosing American Airlines."

My parents had a bad experience on Delta and wrote to them requesting compensation.

> *The flight over was very comfortable with excellent service. We were being picked up by our cruise personnel. . . .*
>
> *On the return trip, however, after we were seated and ready for take off, the pilot informed us that there would be at least an hour's delay but that he was phoning ahead to have our connecting flights aware of our delay.*

We arrived an hour late, but still time to make our plane. There were no porters to help with luggage—we needed two wagons before customs, and by the time we got to the counter to change our tickets all tickets were sold. This was our final outrage. There should have been coordination of people and tickets for the final destination. . . .

We waited over five hours for the next flight to WPB.

We were up for more than twenty-four hours. We have just about gotten back to ourselves to inform you of this incident.

We feel Delta has let us down terribly and we await JUST compensation for this horrible ordeal.

Delta's response was gratifying:

My first wish is that the events you described had never occurred. As a gesture of goodwill, I have enclosed a $200.00 Transportation Certificate for you and your wife's use. Terms and conditions are found on the certificate.

We realize that incentives may not erase the negative impact of your past experiences. We also understand that it is our loyal passengers, such as yourself, that make Delta a strong and successful airline. It is my wish that you will continue to allow Delta Air Lines to be your airline of choice.

There is no standard policy on obtaining customer service either among airlines or within them, for that matter. You cannot reach American's Customer Service Department by phone. They will only accept written requests. Continental, on the other hand, has an 800 number for their Customer Care Department. One of their agents was able to waive our change fees over the phone when another illness caused us to cancel a trip.

As to airline change fees in general. Always ask—"Can you waive this?" I've had them say anything from "Okay" to "You want me to waive this just because you asked?" My answer, "Yes," because I know from experience they have the discretion to do so.

SO:

* There's no standard policy among or within airlines on fee waiving, ticket reimbursement or other issues involving money—and, a "policy" you encounter one day may change the next, or with the next agent you speak to. So, if you don't like what "Michele" has to say, call later and talk to "Tracey."
* If calls don't work, write a letter. Airlines, in particular, are a thousand times more responsive to letters than they are over the phone—unlike the case with other industries.
* Persistence and a determination that you *will* find a way, are what it takes.

7.
Asking Service People for Help

By service people, I mean employees of companies that supply services. They could be household repair companies, automobile repair people, someone at the other end of the 800 number at a bank, a newspaper delivery service, or a flight attendant. It's easy to get spectacular results by simply asking for help. Service people have a lot more discretion than we realize.

Less Is More

If you're carrying a credit card balance at a high-interest rate, call the credit card company and ask them to lower your rate. It's that easy. Just Ask. They'll do it if you persist because they know you can switch to a card with a lower rate, and they don't want to lose your business. It's more profitable for them to retain a customer than to find a new one. Jenelle Barlow and Claus Møller in *A Complaint Is a Gift,* writing about credit card companies note that "for every year customers are retained they represent more in profits because marketing expenses can be amortized against long-term sales results."[1] They go on to say that "if it costs $100 for a company to acquire a new account, then over ten years the cost is $10 per year. Banks also report that the longer credit card customers stay with them, the more likely they are to pay their bills. As well as lower per-unit marketing costs, loss and delinquency ratios improve with customer retention. 'As a result of these figures, some banks reduce rates and fees to their long-term customers, thereby holding on to them for longer periods of time.'"[2]

Credit card companies will also waive annual fees. But you have to Ask. You don't have to give a reason or an argument. Just ask, "Will you waive the annual fee?" You may have to speak with a supervisor or even threaten to cancel the card, but you'll often have success. To retain my business, credit card companies have sent me merchandise credit, frequent-flyer miles, or have simply waived the fee.

Away on vacation and late paying a bill? If you have a good payment record, all you need to do is ask. They'll waive the finance charges.

As for larger charges like check-canceling fees, electronic transfers, late charges on credit cards, ask the question, "Can you waive this fee?" That's all. Don't give an explanation, justification, or hard-luck story. Just ask. This is another instance where front-line people have discretion. Fifty percent of the time, they've said yes.

SO:

- Credit card operators have discretion to waive charges. They can waive annual fees and lower your interest rate.
- Credit card companies don't want to lose our business because it costs them more to acquire new business.
- Mention that you're a long-term customer; you'll get better service.
- Ask them to waive the larger fees on things like check canceling, electronic transfers, and late-payment charges.

Service with a Smile

When we moved into our new house, we decided to get our heating ducts cleaned—maybe it would help with sinuses and allergies. Was this a real or imaginary process? And who to use? There were ads in the paper for $69, yet a large, highly recommended heating and air-conditioning company charged $395. (I checked them out with the Better Business Bureau and they not only had high ratings for many years, but they'd won last year's award for the best company in San Diego.)

It might be money thrown down the drain, but if so, it might as well be a lot. We decided to use the expensive company but ask them for a lower price since we were considering hiring them to install air-conditioning. They knocked off $100. Just like that. I'll say it again: Service people have a lot more discretion than we realize. You don't have to accept the first price they quote. They're usually willing to give you a lower price, but you have to ask.

(Did the duct cleaning work? Who knows.)

• • •

About a month after moving into our new home, the weather turned cold. We switched on the heat. It ran for thirty seconds, went off, ran for thirty seconds, went off.

I called the expensive company. The anticipator (don't ask) was set wrong, the repairman said. He moved the lever up. The whole operation took five minutes, but the bill was $92. You can imagine my surprise!

"That seems like a lot," I said. "Can you help me out?" No reasons given, no hard-luck stories. I just asked.

"Tell you what," he said. "I'll call it a service visit and charge you $45. Is that okay?" It certainly was and seemed much more in line with the work that had been done.

"You see," he confided, "they give us complete discretion on what to charge."

When we were ready to have air-conditioning installed, we got a few estimates—one from the large company and two from smaller companies. The estimates from the smaller companies were about $300 lower than the one from the large company. I checked with the Better Business Bureau again and learned that the little companies hadn't even been rated. We were willing to pay for reliability and track record, so we decided to go with the large company. However . . . it couldn't hurt to ask.

I called the sales rep and told him we'd like to have his company do the job, but we'd received lower estimates.

"Who gave you the other estimates?" he asked.

This was tricky. I knew if I gave him the names, it would be easy for him to attack the smaller companies—and I'd have to agree with him, so I simply said, "I'd rather not say." A question doesn't have to be answered. "But the other estimates were considerably lower," I continued, "so I was hoping you could give us a better price."

"I'll have to consult with my boss," he said.

A few minutes later he called back to say they could knock $150 off the price. The whole negotiation took two minutes. The tone was pleasant, the work done, excellent.

You have to be crazy *not* to ask. I was crazy until very recently. It never occurred to me you could negotiate with contractors.

SO:

+ You can negotiate with service people.
+ It's worth paying more for a reputable company.
+ If you don't like the price, ask for a better one.
+ A question doesn't have to be answered.
+ Service people want you to be happy. Tell them how they can help you. If they can help you, it makes you both feel good.

It's News to Me

The third time I called to report a wet newspaper, I asked for a free month's paper to compensate me for my inconvenience. (At first I thought I'd ask for a week but then thought, why not ask for a month, they can only say no.)

"Okay," the woman said, "we'll give you an extra month at no charge."

If I'm gonna get 'em soggy, they might as well be free.

Last year, that same newspaper, sent me a renewal bill for a year's subscription that seemed rather high. I called Circulation and they said that the yearly rate had gone up from $95 to 124.80 (a nice round number). I asked if they could help me out and give it to me for less—no whining, excuses, complaining—just asking. After a short discussion with a supervisor, I was told I could have it at the previous year's rate. The same thing happened this year. A simple phone call saved me $35 each time.

SO:

- Like your time, your inconvenience is worth something. Ask for compensation when you're inconvenienced.
- You can negotiate on subscriptions.

Half-Asked

Sometimes, in the process of asking, I haven't gone far enough; I either didn't ask for enough or should have taken my request to the next level. I'd be so relieved to receive *any* offer I'd gratefully accept crumbs. We're conditioned to accept the "good enough," but why not go further and keep asking? A first offer is just that—a *first* offer.

One spring night a few years ago, my Toyota Camry emitted a horrible noise, lost its power, and had to be towed to the dealer. The car had only sixty thousand miles and was well cared for.

"It's the transmission," was the chilling diagnosis.

"What will it cost for a new one?" I asked.

"Twenty-nine hundred dollars," was the verdict. Do I need to tell you, I freaked? I'd bought this car for its reliability and was hoping to keep it a few more years. I called around for other quotes, but they were within the same range. (Some people won't go near dealerships for repairs, but you have some leverage with a dealer: a Customer Service Department exists, there are 800 numbers, and the shop stays in business for the life of the repair.)

"Look," I said to the service manager, "I've had all my repairs done by you—everything you recommended. This shouldn't have happened. How can you help me?"

"We'll do it for $1,500," he said. Without blinking an eye, he dropped $1,400 off the price. I took it. But you know what? I should have gone further. I was so relieved, I forgot a first offer is only a first offer. I should have called Toyota Customer Service. Who knows? They may have replaced the transmission for free. It's possible. With all the amazing things that have fallen into my lap since I took Asking full-scale, it wouldn't surprise me.

This was an example of settling. I was so grateful to get *any* offer that I settled for the first offer. I don't do that these days.

SO:

- If you purchased something for its reliability, you have a right to hold the manufacturer responsible if the product doesn't hold up. (Or any other quality that they advertise.)
- Again, a first offer is just that—a *first* offer.
- Don't settle for less than you deserve because you're grateful to get any offer at all.

The Friendly Skies

Ask! can be about improving your situation in intangible ways—your comfort, your state of mind. My friend Stel had to make a last-minute trip across country. Stel has a mild case of claustrophobia. Normally, she's careful to get an aisle seat, but only middle seats were left.

The United Airlines plane was a huge airbus. Mr. Big Body took the seat in front of her and even before he depressed the recline lever, his weight alone pushed his seat toward her. Once in the air, he reclined the seat completely, and his head was nearly in her lap. Stel began to sweat. She felt like she was trapped in a giant MRI. Hyperventilation followed. She frantically summoned the flight attendant and gasped, "Whifty, I'm feeling whifty."

The female attendant acted quickly. "Come with me," she said. She led Stel through the first-class section to the galley. There she tied an apron around Stel's waist. "If you're going to be up here," she said, "you'll have to work."

Stel was on her feet for five hours serving large quantities of alcohol and full-course dinners to the first-class passengers, who she got to know by name. Whether this was company procedure or an inventive flight attendant, it was a wonderful way to diffuse a difficult situation. Stel's panic vanished and didn't reappear even when the plane lurched and she had to go chasing after the serving cart. (They'd forgotten to tell her it had brakes.) For her good work, she was fed a first-class dinner and presented with a bottle of champagne.

As the plane landed, the flight attendant got on the loud-speaker. "We want to thank Stel," she said, "a woman who had a slight problem but was able to work it out by helping others." Cheers came from the first-class section.

Stel's example helped me when I got plunked into the worst seat on the plane because of an itinerary change—the window seat in the last row which *doesn't* recline, so you're really locked in. The same Mr. Big Body sat down in front of me and reclined his seat into my lap. *My* claustrophobia got going, and I rang the flight attendant's bell.

"I have claustrophobia," I told her.

Unfortunately, this wasn't United, and I didn't get whisked off to first-class; but I *did* get switched to an aisle seat in the mid-dle of the plane—leg room and breathing room—something supposedly *not* available when I'd gotten my boarding pass.

Sometimes Asking means showing your vulnerability.

SO:

- Don't be afraid to ask for what you need, anytime, anywhere.
- It's okay to show your vulnerability.

The Infrequent-Flier's Frequent-Flier Miles

This is a story about getting help in two of the most unlikely places—the airlines and the long-distance phone carriers. Even within these industries, not thought of to be customer friendly, you can make real human contacts and get help from individuals. In January 1999, we decided to take a trip to France the following June. We hoped to be able to get tickets with our frequent-flier miles. My new husband and I have a lot in common. When we met, as strange as it sounds, we each had forty thousand American Airlines frequent-flier miles. What are the chances of that? The perfect couple. Just what we needed to go to Europe, or so we thought. But American charges *sixty thousand* miles for flights during the summer. Purchasing tickets would have cost $948 each. Not a good alternative.

A helpful reservation agent told me about the reduced-mileage program. With fifty thousand miles, you pay $225 for a ticket. (Most airlines have reduced-mileage awards, so if you're *almost* there, call and ask.) Fifty thousand miles might be possible to accumulate. We were collecting miles with our MCI accounts—five miles for every dollar you spend—and my husband was about to buy a new car. If he charged it on his Citibank

AAdvantage card—a mile for every dollar—the twenty thousand bonus points would get one of us to our sixty-thousand-mile goal. We called the dealer and were assured we could charge the car. It seemed too good to be true. And it was. When we were ready to pay for the car, he told us we could only charge $3,000, claiming that's what he'd said on the phone. They had us. My husband's old car had gotten us to the dealer, but would it get us home? (More about car salesmen later.)

In a month, we had fifty thousand miles each by charging *everything,* even purchases under $5. (During the months of accumulating mileage, at my request, American extended our redemption date month by month to give us more time.)

Then we received checks from AT&T to entice us to switch from MCI—$100 for my husband, $50 for me. (Sexism, or what?) Since it seemed like we'd never make it to 60,000 miles, we cashed the checks and switched to AT&T. (By the way, I got nowhere with AT&T when I questioned the inequity of the amounts.)

A week later my husband received a call from MCI offering him five thousand miles to switch back. He switched. Then I called about my account, and they gave me a choice of five thousand miles or $75. Since I figured I'd never make the sixty thousand miles, I opted for the money. Seventy-five dollars would help pay the $225 reduced-mileage fee.

But a few days later, we decided to take a last-minute trip to Florida. With the mileage from the Florida trip, I *could* reach sixty thousand miles, except I wouldn't because I'd opted for the $75 instead of the miles.

Making Your Insomnia Work for You

That night, I couldn't sleep, and after tossing for a while, I went into my office and called MCI. The middle of the night is a great time to call airlines, phone companies, mail-order businesses. You get right through. No waits. That's how I make my insomnia work for me.

As I was dialing, I noticed my husband standing in the doorway. He'd "seen the light" and come to see what I was up to.

"I wonder if you can help me," I was saying to the MCI operator. "I goofed by taking $75 instead of five thousand miles, and now were trying to go to France. Could I send the money back and get the miles?"

"France, you're going to France!" the operator said. "I just got back from France. It was wonderful." For the next few minutes, she talked about her trip and recommended places we should see.

"I'll tell you what," she said. "I'm going to do something for you, but you can't tell anyone. I'm going to give you twenty-five thousand miles—five thousand a month for five months, so that you can go to France. I'll give you the code in case you have trouble with the mileage credits." She gave me an award code for a twenty-five-thousand frequent-flyer-mile award for American Platinum Club members.

I got off the phone in shock. My husband stood there shaking his head. We couldn't believe it. He was beginning to think I had special powers.

Unfortunately, by purchase time, I was still 2,995 miles short.

So here I was, 57,005 miles to France. We'd still have to pay the $225 for my ticket after all this work. Well . . . it wouldn't hurt to ask American if they had any suggestions.

When I explained the situation to a sales agent and asked for her help, she said, "No problem; we'll lend you the miles." Again gleeful shock.

So we got help both from service people at American *and* helpful individuals at MCI.

In researching this book, I called American to find out exactly what their mileage-loan policy was. The answer was vague and didn't jibe with what had actually happened, but here it is. American will "consider"—their word—lending miles to people with *active* frequent-flyer accounts. There's no fee for a loan of 500 miles or less, from 501 to 2,500, they charge $25, and from 2,501 to 5,000 miles—the maximum they'll lend— there's a fee of $50. Don't forget to ask them to waive *these* fees. No fee was mentioned when they loaned me the 2,995 miles.

Other airlines have similar policies but these policies shift depending on who you talk with and what the weather's like. Keep asking till you get an answer you like.

My mileage collecting is penny ante compared to the guy in Sacramento who amassed 1.25 million miles by purchasing Healthy Choice diet pudding. In the spring of 1999, Dave Phillips discovered that Healthy Choice awarded one thousand frequent-flyer miles for every ten UPC labels.[3] He figured that at 25 cents each, Healthy Choice pudding cups were the most economical way to earn the miles. So for every $2.50, he earned one thousand miles. Since most carriers charge you twenty-five thousand for domestic flights, the pudding labels would get him a ticket for $62.50—and all that yummy pudding. To fly to Europe at forty thousand miles would cost $100. Dave invested $3,140 in pudding for flights worth $25,000—enough to take him around the world forty-eight times. (A lot of packing there.) This amounted to twelve thousand cups of diet pudding. That's *some* diet. In this calculation, what's lacking are the labor costs. At the peak of label peeling, Dave says he "could do four hundred labels an hour" which bought twenty-four thousand miles. Can you get a repetitive stress injury from all this peeling? He ran out of time and had to donate—i.e., tax deduction—the pudding to the Salvation Army and other food banks, but he did so with the stipulation that they peel the labels. (Every soup kitchen in Sacramento now serves pudding for dessert.)

The frequent-flier coupons showed up "without fanfare." "The *Wall Street Journal* . . . quoted an official of Healthy Choice as saying the frequent-flier offer 'met and exceeded expectations,' although the company's spokeswoman wouldn't discuss the promotion's sales figures or data about participants." Nor their need for smelling salts.

SO:

- Regulations are meant to be questioned—often they're surprisingly flexible.
- Airline personnel—*and* long-distance service people have a lot of discretion. They can award you miles, extend ticket-redemption dates, and lend you miles.
- Call twenty-four-hour businesses at off-hours for quicker service.
- Keep asking. If you don't get an answer you like, call back and talk with the next operator. Policies are flexible or nonexistent.

Asking for Trouble

Sometimes, *asking* is exactly the wrong thing to do—it can open up the proverbial can of worms and cause unnecessary trouble. This is something I've learned from my husband. The disparity in our styles showed up on our trip to France. We rented a large, expensive car—a Mercedes, in fact—to protect us from European drivers. What we hadn't counted on was that we'd also need protection from European parking lots.

The first time we backed into a below-the-vision impediment was in a parking garage in Lyon. The garage was so vast and cleverly planned that it had actually won architectural awards. The design was a double helix that tunneled deep into the earth. When you looked over the edge, there was no bottom.

Fortunately, the Mercedes had a thick, black, rubber guard over the bumper. Only the rubber was scratched—but the car no longer looked mint. Next, we backed into another "invisible" impediment in the charming, preauto village of Cliousclat. Another scratch on the bumper. On top of that, someone crashed into us in the rain in Montpellier. Glass shattered, brakes screeched—the other driver sped away. Fortunately it wasn't *our* glass or *our* brakes, just another abrasion on the black bumper. Our finale was backing into yet another small, concrete "nubbin" in a parking garage in center-city Montpellier. Yes, we're slow learners. (In these old cities not intended to accommodate cars, they hide them underground. My next book will be called, *A Year **Under** Provence.*)

Early childhood experiences at Coney Island on the Bumper Car Ride hadn't prepared us for this, but there *was* a distinct similarity. Though weren't those bumper car rides actually fun?

On our drive to the airport to return the car, we debated about how to handle these little thingys? I suggested that we ask the rental agency if the scratches were a problem, and if so contact our insurance company and get it over with, rather than have the agency chasing after us.

My husband was appalled. Was I crazy? The little scratches on the rubber strip hardly constituted damage. Look around, he said. All the other cars have similar dingys. This was totally expected in Europe; but if we pointed it out, we would surely be held responsible. He was very upset. Adamant, in fact. Asking in this situation would have netted us anything but help.

Well, I'd never rented a car in Europe so I agreed to handle it his way. He actually asked me to wait outside while he returned the car.

(Finding the rental agency was another matter. Yes, we could see it in the rental car area, but the only entrance was marked with a DO NOT ENTER sign. After two passes around the airport, we decided to disobey and enter. Later, we learned from someone staying at our hotel, that this *was* the way to enter. When in Rome . . .)

As agreed, I remained outside while my husband returned the car. The rental agent gave the car a quick once-over and wished us bon voyage. I ate crow soup for dinner.

SO:

- Don't ask for trouble.
- When driving in France, or, especially parking, beware of concrete nubbins.

Enough to Drive You Crazy

An area that we've already touched on is the car purchase. This is a place where you definitely *won't* get help from salespeople. In fact, you need to question and requestion anything they promise you, then get it in writing. (Remember the twenty thousand frequent-flier miles we were hoping for when my husband bought his car; that shrank to three thousand?)

Often, car buying is a back-against-the-wall decision. If your old car's on its last legs, or even DOA, you're under tremendous pressure. You know you need a car, and stuff can slip past you. Relieve the pressure on yourself by getting a rental car for as long as you need one so you can make a careful decision. You'll own your new car for three to seven years, (an *observation,* not a statistic), so $25 a day for a rental car is a teeny price to pay for such a big decision.

And just like going to the doctor for a serious problem, take someone with you to buy a car. You'll always forget something—the upgraded stereo speakers, the floor mats—how about a clock? Many inexpensive cars today come without clocks. Who would think to ask? *I* always forget to negotiate a loaner-car for repairs, which is really important to me because of my ungodly dread of being carless.

Something I've noticed in my car-buying experiences is that car salesmen are poor mathematicians—they often make mistakes in *their* favor. It's happened to me three times. The first math-deficient salesman was a crusty old geezer who tried to create a sense of trustworthiness by being "down-home." He almost succeeded. When he "couldn't find" his calculator and started adding up the figures in his head, I offered *my* calculator. But he tapped his arithmetic head and waved away my HP.

"Best calculator's in here," he said warmly.

It turned out not. When I checked the figures with my "second best" calculator, I discovered he was $500 off, not, as you might guess, in my favor.

Years later, another salesman tried to sell me on trusting his head. His remarkable head was off by $100. (Guess in whose favor?) There's a theme here.

Even computers owned by car dealers are not so hot at math, but computer-generated sales sheets look so official, they're enough to intimidate you. The pressure's on. The sales team has put you through it. So when the final papers come, you want to sign and get out of there. But take a minute to read them. When my husband bought his car, the computer "forgot" to include the $2,500 factory rebate and the $1,500 dealer rebate. When he pointed out the omissions to the salesman, the salesman said, "Oops," and whisked the contract away to get it "corrected." There was a strong, fishy odor in the air.

My husband says that when he buys a car, he expects to be (1) inconvenienced, (2) humiliated, and (3) cheated in the process. If only two out of three happens, he considers it a successful transaction.

SO:

- Take the pressure off yourself and get a rental car when you're purchasing a new car.
- Bring someone along with you when you buy a car. Two heads might remember all the things you wanted to negotiate for.
- Remember: Car salesmen can't add. Double-check their calculations.
- Read the contract. Computers in car dealerships don't seem to work all that well.

8.

Finding Opportunities for Asking in Unexpected Places

We've already seen a number of unexpected opportunities for asking. Who would think to ask a dentist for a refund, a veterinarian for a senior discount, the interest rate on a CD to be raised? Here are a bunch more unusual opportunities for asking. Some of them I discovered the hard way—by *not* realizing I could ask for something readily available. Reading these stories will expand your awareness of the surprising places Asks are lurking. Soon you'll come up with your own astonishing Asks.

Elopement, Sr.

I'm still kicking myself for *not* asking. A few weeks after we returned from France, we decided to get married. We snuck off to City Hall and were married by a clerk of the court. It was surprising how much everything cost. A marriage license used to be $3. Today it's $50. And the civil ceremony, another $50.

As we were leaving the courthouse, I said to my new husband, "Damn, I should have asked for a senior discount."

Discontinued or Obsolete

You've found the perfect lipstick, bra, shoes, shampoo . . . The next time you try to buy it, you're told it's been discontinued. I have hard-to-fit, quirky feet, so when I found a pair of shoes that were not only comfortable but nice-looking, too, I went back to the store for another pair.

But I was too late. They were last season's style, I was told. The store no longer carried them. *Fashion strikes again.* I asked the saleswoman to call their other stores. She tried, but the shoes were gone. They'd been shipped back to the factory to make room for this season's styles.

I was desperate. I called the main office. Maybe I could I buy the shoes from the factory.

"Help!" I said, after I'd voice mailed my way up to the head buyer.

"I'm sorry," she said, "this style is no longer for sale."

"But, but, but . . . , do you have any lying around?"

"Let me look," she said. When she came back a few minutes later, she had good news. "Actually, we have two pairs in your size—one in black patent and one in bone."

"Oh, thank God," I said. "Should I send you a check?"

"I can't sell them to you," she said, "this isn't a sales office. We have no facility for taking money. . . . Tell you what, I'll just send them to you."

I'm still wearing these shoes—*very carefully.*

Something similar happened to my daughter Julie. My parents had handed down to her a perfectly good TV—perfectly good, that is, except for one problem: they'd misplaced the remote and the TV was frozen on close-captioning, which took up a quarter of the screen. No manipulation of buttons would remove it.

Julie took the set to a large electronic store for help, but no one there could solve the problem. They suggested calling the manufacturer, JVC, and buying a remote from them.

She called JVC and explained the problem. The guy at the other end of the 800 number said he'd check to see what he had. He searched the computer and came up with one for $75.

"I hate to spend $75 on such an old set," she said.

He searched some more and came up with one for $30, but he couldn't guarantee that it was compatible with her set.

"Even $30 seems like a lot if you don't know whether it will work."

"Tell you what," he said, "I'll just send it to you."

If you don't ask . . .

We don't give up easily in my family.

SO:

- If you like something that's fashion dependent like shoes, hurry up and buy a few pairs.
- Be persistent. If one way doesn't work, keep looking for another.

Waive for Me

Sometimes we *don't* ask because we make incorrect assumptions. Assumptions cause trouble, assumptions based on tradition, habit, and custom. Because things have "always been" a certain way, we assume that's the way they still are. Yet if you don't ask, you risk missing out on what's readily available just for the Asking.

A few years ago I went for acupuncture treatments. I *assumed* my insurance wouldn't cover them, so I didn't bother asking. Months later a friend mentioned *she* was getting acupuncture, and her insurance company was paying for most of it. And we had the same insurance! I ran home and called the company, but I was too late. Anything beyond six months wasn't covered. That was a negative $600 assumption.

My friend Ellen E-mailed me about a costly assumption she'd made:

> *Sat, 4 Dec 1999 19:58:30-0700*
> *Hi Barbara,*
> *I've been thinking about your book and remembered a time when I didn't ask: When I went through an employment agency in 1981 to get my job*

at ———————, where I headed the accounting dept. for 14 years, it never occurred to me to ask the company to pay the fee, which was 10% of a year's salary——a significant amount for me as a single parent! After being there a couple years, I was chatting with a woman from Human Resources who had become my good friend, and somehow the topic of this fee came up. She told me that if I had asked when I was hired, the company would have paid it! I'm sure that experience helped me be more vigilant about asking . . .
Ellen

In both cases, all we needed to do was ask and we could have received benefits that were **available to everyone.** These are two examples of situations where nobody was trying to cheat us or block us—we talked ourselves out of asking by making incorrect assumptions. I've included them to raise awareness of yet more nooks and crannies where Asks are hiding. I've since learned to Always Ask: to have a fee waived, to have someone else pay it, to be reimbursed.

SO:

• Assumptions can prevent us from getting what's readily available if we had asked. Don't assume anything. Ask.
• When you see the word "fee," think "waive."

Quickies

Change of Address

Goodies hide in unusual places. The change-of-address packets from the post office often contain valuable coupons—for 10 percent off an entire purchase at Home Depot or maybe $5 off a purchase at Sears. These coupons have no stipulations—you don't have to move—and you can pick up as many packets as you like.

Compliments, Compliments

When compliments are due, I pay them. On a trip during the Christmas holidays, *I* arrived but my luggage didn't. The people at USAir handled the situation expeditiously and courteously, and I wasn't long without my luggage.

I wrote to Customer Service, thanking them and naming the people who'd helped me. USAir responded by sending me coupons for two upgrades, two drink vouchers, and a thousand frequent-flyer miles on my next two trips. Pretty nice.

• • •

The salesperson who sold us the wicker chairs at Pier 1 Imports undercharged us by $80. I pointed out the mistake, and she gratefully redid the sale. To tell the truth, my honesty wasn't motivated by concern for Pier 1's profits, but rather by concern that the salesperson would be penalized. This is an instance where personal ethics motivated my behavior.

I also compliment anyone who's working for me and doing a good job—usually these are people in thankless tasks like house cleaners, lawyers, real estate agents, rental management companies. They deserve it, and it gets you remembered. It may be the only compliment they receive all year.

You Rub My Back, I'll Rub Yours

Barter is a great way to extend the dollar. It's more tricky and subtle than it used to be, but if you stay on your toes, you can come up with a way. Think about what skills or services you have to offer.

Several years ago, I was getting massage therapy for computer-stress relief. A few sessions in, the therapist mentioned he was trying to sell his home himself. After the massage, he bombarded me with questions since he knew I'd been in real estate.

"I have an idea," I said, "How about we exchange real estate advice for free massages?"

He thought it was a great idea. Of course it was tricky. How do you sort out what's fair? But we were both satisfied with the arrangement, and the stakes were low. I got some free massages, and he got some free advice. (You know how much *that's* worth.)

SO:

- It's okay to be stingy with money, but be generous with compliments. They make the world a better place.
- Stay on your toes. Opportunities are abundant for the observant.

9.
Asking for
Warrantees to Work

"This product comes with a lifetime guarantee." Sounds good, doesn't it. Often you'll see such a promise on trivial items—things under $5 you'd never think of returning. There *are* those who file away warrantees. I had an uncle who never had to buy a new garden hose. Years ago, before records were kept, he bought some hoses with ten-year warrantees. He kept the warrantees in a file—since donated to the Smithsonian. No hose ever lasted the ten years, so every now and then he'd show up at Sears with the decaying hoses—water dripping in his wake—for his replacements. This practice went on for over *forty* years.

Whose Lifetime Is It Anyway?

My cousin Gina bought a set of silverplate because it carried a lifetime guarantee of resilvering at no charge at any time. After thirty years of use, the set needed resilvering. She'd kept the original paperwork, including the lifetime guarantee, so when she contacted the company, she expected an easy transaction.

But alas, all things change. The company had been bought out. "We don't do that sort of thing," the new company told her. **Yet they were still selling silverplate under the original name.** Don't warranties convey in a sale or merger, especially if they're still doing business *under the same name?*

Gina is *thinking* of writing to the CEO of the new company. Why not call? I ask. No, she'll put it all in a letter when she gets around to it.

Lots of people *think* of writing. Scads of wonderful letters get written in people's heads. Few get committed to paper. My money's *not* on Gina. By the time she gets around to writing, we'll be worrying about Y3K.

Calling is immediate. You can address the problem while you're in the thick of it and still passionate about it. And you have a chance of making a real human connection. My husband says a major reason for my successes is that I establish a relationship with the person at the other end of the line.

As you climb the corporate ladder, keep asking, "and who's *your* boss?" If you can't get anyone to help you on the phone, it may be that writing won't accomplish anything either, and you've thrown good time after bad. What's happened is, you've run into a business that isn't terribly concerned about their most important asset, you, the customer.

So if your complaint is stalled because you think you have to write a letter and can't get yourself to do it, you're off the hook. Call instead.

For some, though, letter writing is still the method of choice, and there are services on the Internet that will write the letter for you—usually for a fee: sites such as *www.complain .com, www.fightback.com, www.cemptor.com* (for caveat emptor), *www.ellensPoisonPen.com.*

SO:

+ In the rapidly changing world of business, "lifetime guarantees" may not be worth the paper they're written on.
+ Call, don't write; you're more likely to *do* it. Most letters never get committed to paper.
+ If you don't get the answer you need, ask for a person with more authority.

Those Mysterious Noises Again

Another case of Customer Noise Delusion? That's what a large electronics store wanted me to believe about my top-of-the-line, twenty-seven-inch TV set. When I first bought the set, it made mild "settling" noises soon after I turned it on. Gradually, over the year, the noises got worse, becoming more frequent and louder.

Though I rarely buy extended warranties, their warranty covered in-home service and I knew I could never carry the twenty-seven-inch thing to a repair shop, so I paid $89 for a three-year warranty. I got lucky this time, or unlucky, since I had quite a hassle getting the thing fixed.

"That's normal," was the Customer Service verdict about the noise, "due to expansion and contraction."

"I've never heard anything like it before," I said.

"That's because the new TVs are all plastic. It's the plastic." What were they made of before, kryptonite?

Over the next few months, the noise increased from a mild annoyance to a real problem. I asked them to check it out. Their first in-home repair did nothing. The second visit made it worse: The TV now made loud, cracking noises at random times, whether on *or* off. It got so bad that it often startled me awake in the middle of the night.

I escalated, as I should have done long before—but they had me believing it was me, not them. I was being too picky, they implied. The emperor had clothes. The head of the repair department told me, "All Panasonics do this."

Soon after repair number two, I visited my son and his wife, and I realized that they had the same TV. (Apparently, there's a genetic predisposition to purchase this exact TV.)

"Does your TV make cracking noises?" I asked them.

"What?" They looked at me as if I were mad.

That did it. I insisted that the store either fix this TV or give me a new one. They said they would take it into the shop. (Would you believe I had to pry a loaner out of them? You would.) They worked on it a week—*I* had to make the call to get the thing back. They'd taken it apart, they said, cleaned it, and put insulating tape at the seams. And guess what? It's never made a peep since. Evidently not *all* Panasonics make this noise. Mine doesn't anymore.

SO:

+ Don't be intimidated by the "It's not us, it's you" tactic.
+ Be persistent.
+ Ask questions.
+ While your appliance is in the shop, ask for a loaner.

Business as Unusual

This is a story about the dizzying rate of change in both the marketplace and technology. You'll need a scorecard. A few years ago, I bought a discontinued Canon laptop for $1,300, about a third less than comparable laptops. I purchased a three-year CompUSA warranty. (Scare tactics worked on me; laptops are fragile, etc., etc.) And it turned out to be a good thing because after eight months, the laptop needed a new motherboard. It's weird, though, to have a three-year warranty on a computer. After three years, the thing is extinct. Repairing it is like bringing a dinosaur in for a tune-up.

As it turned out, I rarely traveled with the laptop and instead used it as a hard drive, attaching peripherals—monitor, mouse, keyboard, printer. Coincidentally, a month before the three-year warranty was up, I bought an up-to-date CPU to replace the now obsolete laptop, figuring I'd use the laptop for the purpose for which it was intended and take it on trips. The problem with this plan was that the battery didn't charge.

I called the Canon parts department to order a new battery, but they gave me another number to call. Now here's where you need to take out your scorecard. I called the new number and reached a company called Decision One. A woman informed me that the problem was probably with the battery charger, *not* the battery, because this was a common problem with the model I had.

Luckily, I still had a month left on my warranty. I called the number on the CompUSA warranty card. Notice the wording I use. This was the brochure I'd been given when I bought the computer three years before. Evidently, a lot had happened in these three years. The person at the other end of the line said they'd send a carton for the laptop and have UPS pick it up. Ten days later the laptop was back, but the battery still didn't work. Assuming the charger had been fixed, the problem had to be with the battery.

So I called Decision One and ordered a new battery. With shipping, it cost $108, which I charged on my Visa. But the new battery didn't help. I called Decision One and they give me the "It's not us, it's you" response. CompUSA didn't know how to fix the charger, they claimed, but they, Decision One, would be glad to repair it for $85. At this point, I realized that only face-to-face contact could help me out of this morass, so I packed up the laptop, marched into CompUSA, and asked to speak to the manager. When I told him I'd sent the laptop to their warranty service and it hadn't been fixed, he shook his head.

"We stopped using that warranty service a few years ago," he said. "There were too many complaints." This was getting weird. The server, it turned out, was merely a subcontractor of Comp-USA, who now no longer used them. Why didn't someone tell *me?* It was certainly information I could have used. The manager said they would try to fix it in-store, but he had his doubts.

It was so strange—the old service contractor had sent me a box and claimed to fix the laptop, yet they were no longer affiliated with CompUSA. I'll never understand why they had gone to the trouble and expense. There must have been tons of complaints for CompUSA to cancel the contract. I searched the Internet to see if I could learn something about this situation. What I discovered was that CompUSA had recently been sold to a Mexican corporation. Had *anything* stayed the same? Would they change the name to CompMEXICO?

A few days later, a CompUSA technician called me. They couldn't fix it, he said, but they would give me a new CompUSA laptop instead. That was great. They replaced the Canon with an inexpensive laptop, but far better than anything three-years-old.

The next thing wrong with this picture was that I was stuck with an unused $108 battery for a laptop I no longer possessed. I called Decision One and told them I wanted to return the battery. No returns, they said, that was their "policy." They had told me so, they insisted. Not only hadn't they told me, but there was nothing on their invoice to indicate this policy.

I asked the CompUSA manager for help. There was nothing he could do, he said. Why don't I take it up with Visa, he suggested. Well, I was weary and I'd just gotten a brand-new computer from CompUSA, so I decided that when I had the energy, I would pursue it with Visa. My husband said, forget it.

"Look at it this way. You got a new laptop for $100. And time is money," he reminded me. But I was pissed. I decided to give it one shot, then forget it.

My husband was also concerned I could mess up our credit by getting into a dispute, so I checked out the procedure before filing a complaint. According to the statement on the back of the Visa bill, "You do not have to pay any amount in question while we are investigating, but you are still obligated to pay the parts of your bill that are not in question. While we investigate your question, we cannot report you as delinquent on the disputed item or take any action to collect the amount you question."

They go on to say that you must inform them of a problem within sixty days of incurring the charge, either by phone or by completing the form on the back of the Visa bill.

When I contacted them, I was told I must attempt to return the product and forward Visa a copy of the mail receipt before they would act. Visa gave me a temporary credit of $108 while they put the matter into dispute. So I packed up the battery and sent it registered to Decision One.

A few days later, the battery was bounced back to me with a note written on a copy of my receipt. They didn't take back electronic items, it said, but they would be glad to repair the laptop for $85. I sent a copy to Visa, pointing out that nowhere on the receipt did it state a nonreturn policy. Then I forgot about the whole thing. Two months later, I received a letter from Visa stating that Decision One had not contested my claim and the dispute was decided in my favor.

In this instance, I felt particularly vindicated.

SO:

* Corporations are changing at an unbelievable rate.
* Bring your old computer to a museum.
* Persistence, persistence, persistence.
* You can contest any practice that you haven't been informed of.
* It's easy to contest a charge on a Visa or Mastercard.

10.
Getting Compensation
from Companies

Sometimes, a product or a service is not only inadequate or defective, it actually causes damage. In these situations it's not enough to be refunded the cost of the item. How about compensation for the damage? We're so relieved to receive a refund, we don't think to ask to be reimbursed for the damage something caused, thereby accepting less than we're entitled to.

A defective service is where something's not delivered in a timely manner, or the service is not what you contracted for—thereby wasting *our* time. The stories that follow are about asking for the complete remedy—a refund and a reimbursement.

A Little Extra Protein?

I noticed some icky bugs crawling up my kitchen walls. Creepy-looking things, they looked like anorexic ticks. A California specialty I was not familiar with? I wiped them up, flushed them down the toilet, and hoped for the best. The next day there were many more, and they were now in the family room. My husband and I swept through and banished them.

The day after more appeared, and one was upstairs in our bedroom. That's it! I had no intention of sharing my bed with these disgusting things. But what to do? We were opposed to pesticides, yet these creatures were gaining on us. It was Friday night and I didn't want to spend the weekend with these uninvited guests. Maybe we could find what they were on the Internet, though it seemed like searching for a tick in a haystack.

I went to *www.dogpile.com,* a multisearch engine, and entered the word "insect." The second or third listing was *www. webhelp.com.* Live help, the site advertised. When I opened it, script appeared with Darin introducing himself. How can he help? he wrote.

"Can you identify a black insect that looks like an unengorged tick?" I answered. My husband and I were both skeptical, and we'd be late for the movies if we fooled around with this much longer. I went to get my coat.

"My, God, there it is!" my husband shouted. I ran back to the computer and there, many times larger than life, was our bug. It was a rice weevil. Webhelp had taken us to the University of Michigan Agricultural Extension Site. We rushed to the pantry where the rice was stored, and sure enough, the weevils were pouring out of a bag of rice. The rice was loose rice straight from an open bin at a health food store, part of a national chain. While my husband mopped up the weevils, I went back to the computer where a question appeared from Darin, "Barbara, did this help you?"

"Yes," I wrote back. "Now, can you tell me how to get rid of them?" In a short time, another site came up with practical instructions on how to eliminate these nasty-looking critters. Mainly, it said, get rid of the source. Get rid of the rice, and they'd have nothing to lay their eggs on. The site also advised putting loose rice in the freezer for four days after purchasing to kill any eggs. In fact the eggs could be eliminated entirely if the store or the supplier froze the rice before putting it out for sale.

"Let's throw out the rice," I said.

"How about bringing them back to the store?" My husband said.

Gulp. "I never thought of that." So instead of going to the movies, we spent the evening cleaning out our kitchen cabinets, tossing anything with rice or wheat, and scrubbing everything down with Lysol.

We double bagged the swarming rice and stuck it in the freezer. The next day we retrieved the mess—still now, no more swarming—and brought it to the supermarket. Yes, the manager said, there are maggots in the rice. I should have stored it in a sealed container, he said accusingly, implying I should have known. This is a common tactic—making it the customer's fault, putting you on the defensive. I've been buying rice a lot of years, and this had never happened before.

"How would *I* know?" I asked. "There's no sign or directions on the rice. Don't you think you ought to warn people how to handle it?"

"That would be a good idea," he acknowledged.

I went on. "We'd like to be compensated for our inconvenience, and for the food we had to throw out."

"I don't suppose a $20 gift certificate would do it?" he asked. He was a bright one.

"No," I agreed.

In that case, he said, I'd have to talk with the "team" manager on Monday.

I waited till Tuesday. Monday is never a good day to pursue problems. Personnel are swamped and less likely to address your problem in a positive manner.

The team manager turned out to be a weak link. A weak link is someone in the chain of command who drops the ball. This one didn't return calls. So I climbed the ladder to the regional manager's office. His assistant clucked over my story and agreed that the stores should post directions on how to handle goods sold in open bins. She'd talk to someone and get back to me.

The next day, she called and offered me a hundred-dollar gift certificate. The $100 would cover the tossed goods and our cleaning time, so I accepted.

I called the California Department of Agriculture and learned that it's standard for rice to contain maggot eggs—and *within* health guidelines. I should store the rice in a sealed container, they said. It seems everyone in the country knew to do this except me. So don't bother eating that chicken breast with the rice. You're getting enough protein *in* the rice.

SO:

- Don't let personnel intimidate you by implying or even saying that "you should have known." They should have *told* you.
- If you buy from open bins, store items in sealed containers and, if it won't ruin the food, freeze it for a few days.
- Make suggestions to businesses on ways to better serve the consumer—like notifying us on how to store a product.
- It's not enough to be refunded for a defective item if the item has damaged something else. Ask to be reimbursed for the damage *and* the time it took to remedy the damage.
- Don't make calls on a Monday.
- A first offer is just that, a *first* offer. Go to the next level and ask for more.
- The Internet is amazing.

Don't Settle for Less

While waiting on line at a discount linen chain, a point-of-purchase item caught my attention. (That's what they're designed to do, "point-of-purchase" is merchandisese for the area around the check-out counter where they put the stuff they want you to buy on impulse. Manufacturers pay premiums to have their merchandise displayed in these prime slots.) This particular item was an enzyme-impregnated cloth advertised to prevent colors from running in the wash.

"It really works!" the kid at the check-out counter enthused when he saw me looking at it.

Well, maybe it did for him, but the pink sweater I washed with the gray towel came out a new color—grink.

"Oh, that's terrible," the clerk said, when I returned with the cloth and the formerly pink top. "We'll be happy to refund your money."

"What about the sweater?" I asked.

"Okay, how about $10?"

"It cost $30, but it's a year old. How about $20?"

"Okay."

SO:

- It's not enough to be refunded for a defective item if the item has damaged something else. Ask to be reimbursed for the damage also.
- Again—a first offer is just a first offer.

Time Is Money

Time is money. We use this worn-out phrase as an excuse for not doing something, but it takes on new force when someone else is in control of our time. Like when delivery and service people are late. It's not only that you have to take time off from work and are stuck in the house. It's the **waiting.** Your life is put on hold. Should I start this project or will the doorbell ring? Should I make this important call, or will the doorbell ring? Should I go to the bathroom? And worst of all, is the dread, the existential dread, that they're never really coming at all.

You call them, and if you're lucky enough to get out of voice-mail hell, you'll be given some vague answer as to the whereabouts of the delivery van. *They're on their way.* From Canada? They were due an hour ago.

But what if businesses were asked to share the burden for our inconvenience? Where it hurts—in the pocket. When my friend Rick bought a washing machine at Sears, they gave him a two-hour delivery window—from 9:00 A.M. to 11:00 A.M., which meant Rick had to take time off from work. The washing machine didn't show up till 1:00 P.M. Rick called Sears and asked them to compensate him $25 an hour for the additional time he'd lost at work. In fact, he mentioned that until they agreed to do so, he wouldn't take delivery on the washer. They said okay and credited his Visa $50.

What a wonderful concept! We *do* have recourse. We don't have to sit there and "take it." Our time is worth something. (*We're* worth something.) Another example proving we have a lot more power than we think.

A few weeks after hearing Rick's story, I went to pick up an etching that I'd had framed. When I got home and removed the wrapping, I saw that the hanger was incorrectly attached—vertically, instead of horizontally. What a pain. I'd have to waste time taking this thing back and waiting for them to correct their mistake. Then I remembered Rick. When I returned to the shop, I asked the manager to compensate me for my inconvenience.

"How much would you like?" he asked.

Frankly, I didn't know. This was the first time I'd asked to get compensated for my time, so I hadn't thought it through. The framing had cost $61.

"Half the cost of the framing," I said.

"I'm afraid I can't do that," he said.

"What *can* you do?"

"Ten dollars," he said. I took it.

Half-hour film developing turned into five hours thanks to a broken machine. When the clerk went to ring up our pictures, I asked, "Shouldn't you give them to us for free for having to wait this long?"

"Okay," she said—with a smile, actually—and handed them to us.

•   •   •

Pier 1 Imports was scheduled to deliver a chair between 10:00 and 2:00—an outrageous time spread, but they wouldn't close the gap. At 1:50, they still hadn't arrived and I had to leave. Not wanting to go through another four-hour wait, I called the store and told them to leave the chair on the front porch. The chair was wicker so, although it was inconvenient, I knew we could carry it upstairs ourselves.

The next day I called the manager. "I wonder if you can help me?" I said. I explained that the delivery men had been late, and we had had to carry the chair upstairs ourselves.

"Oh, that's terrible," she said.

"We'd like to be reimbursed the $45 delivery charge."

"We'll be glad to do that," she said.

I ordered blinds for our new home from Home Expo. The installer said he would come to measure at 4:00 Thursday.

Four o'clock, 4:15, 4:30. I called Expo. A pleasant-sounding young woman, "Sandy," asked me to wait while she called the installer. It seems they were running forty-five minutes to an hour late.

"I wish they'd called," I said.

"They *should* have called," she acknowledged—now that's the kind of opening I like.

I asked to be compensated for my lost time. "At $50 an hour," I said.

"We don't do that," Sandy said.

I thought for a minute; I was so exasperated. This was one in a long line of repair people I'd had to wait for since we'd moved into our new home. So I made a threat—it was foolhardy, but I had had it. "Then cancel my order." I said.

"Oh," Sandy said, "could you hold while I talk to the manager?"

I held.

"We'll credit you $35 for the measuring fee," she said. So it seemed that they *do* do "that." But by now it was now 5:00 P.M., and the installers hadn't *yet* arrived. I dug in my heels.

"I'll take the $35," I said, "but I'll never set foot in your store again."

Would I please hold again?

When she got back on the line, she said, "All right, we'll credit you $50."

The story goes on. Two surfer dudes breeze in at 5:15. They're laughing and kidding. They manage to fit in a little measuring throughout all the fun. Maybe they got *some* measurements right, I hoped. When there's life, there's hope.

The blinds were supposed to be ready in two to three weeks, but at the end of two weeks, Sandy called me. "We'd like to schedule you for a remeasure," she said. "We're using a more reliable company now."

"What!" I had had a *feeling* the Misters Casual weren't for real.

"The blinds won't be ready for another three weeks, but we'll credit you the full cost of the installation, $211.36."

My son Michael rented a truck to pick up a new washer and dryer at a warehouse club. He'd called the nearest branch to make certain they had the models he wanted, but when he arrived, the washer and dryer could not be found. The manager was very apologetic and located the models at another branch. Michael asked to be reimbursed the $50 truck rental costs to compensate him for his inconvenience; the manager agreed without hesitation.

• • •

As you can see, recourse is available just for the Asking. And our successes are not only financially beneficial, they're also psychologically satisfying. They make us feel that we have a voice, that we count, that someone cares about our satisfaction. Maybe if more of us asked to be compensated for our time and inconvenience, businesses would become more responsive.

And because time is money, I *don't* patronize a large computer store in Southern California—although they have the best selection and the best prices. It's their return policy that's the problem. First, you have to wait in line for a "technician," who examines your item and grills you on what's wrong with it, what *you've* done to it. That takes at least a half hour. Then he'll offer a replacement—and take ten minutes to find it. Finally, if you get through *that* line, and your return is approved, you have to wait on another line to get your refund. I went through *that* drill once.

They sure discourage returns—both of merchandise *and* of customers.

SO:

- Ask to be compensated for your wasted time and inconvenience.
- Responsible businesses take responsibility for their mistakes.
- Vote with your feet. Don't patronize businesses that discourage returns. Patronize businesses that make returns easy.
- It's worth paying a little more to avoid hassles and waits.

Sail Away

My father could never be described as nonconfrontational. He returns broken items to stores years later, without a receipt, expects to get his money back, and usually does. Recently, he returned a thirty-year-old seltzer maker from Hammacher Schlemmer to another store and they gave him a new one—*for free*. Am I his daughter or what?

But for even the toughest among us, there are times when we're willing to accept the unacceptable. Two years ago I went on a cruise with my parents. My mother was then in her late seventies, my father in his eighties. They look and act a lot younger, but they weren't prepared for the rigorous workout we were treated to as a result of the ship's negligence.

Instead of docking at the pier in Charlotte Amalie, Saint Thomas, as we were scheduled to, the ship dropped anchor a mile out and tendered people to the dock. The reason, we were told, was that there was no room in the harbor. (At the inn?) Strange how two of the line's other ships—those on more expensive, ten-day cruises—were neatly tucked into the harbor. We were supposed to believe that even with electronic communications and years-ahead planning, the cruise line hadn't known about this. The smell of fish hung in the air.

Boarding the tenders was a real challenge. The seas were rough with eight-foot swells. Crew members tossed passengers onto a tender when a swell brought it level with the ship. I wondered out loud at the wisdom of trying to board. My parents pooh-poohed my objections—they'd been on cruises where getting on tenders was much dicier than this. Was I a scaredy-cat or something? They shamed me into silence.

My mother and I were hauled on first, our arms successfully left in our sockets—pure luck, that. My father was next. A second after they got him on the tender, the sea heaved and sent him splat on his back. My mother and I gasped. It looked like something terrible had happened. The man was eighty-four. Miraculously, he ended up with a slight bruise on his back, which bothered him later, but he shrugged the incident off.

The way I saw it, the cruise line was guilty of gross negligence. We should never have been hoisted onto those tenders. In fact, tender service was halted shortly after we left because a passenger actually *fell* into the gap between the two vessels and was barely rescued.

Meanwhile, back at the ranch, throngs of angry passengers—the lucky ones who'd been trapped aboard—bombarded the desk with complaints. As an answer to these complaints, letters were slipped under cabin doors giving $25 ship's credit to each passenger. By dropping anchor a mile out, the letter explained, the line didn't have to pay port charges. Greed seemed to be the motive for not docking. The $25 satisfied *some* passengers; not me.

My father's back was aching, yet I had to press him to get examined by the ship's doctor. My father's attitude was, you can't expect much from cruise lines, and he was lucky not to have sustained permanent damage. (He didn't want to rock the boat?) The doctor gave him Tylenol and a phone number to call when he got home. When he made the call, the cruise line immediately offered him $2,000. He took it. Oh well. *Sic transit gloria.*

My father had this same attitude at my mother's eightieth birthday celebration in Las Vegas. It was October 16, 1999. Our entire family, fourteen of us, were asleep when the Hector Mines earthquake struck. (My mother *does* like having a fuss made over her, but this was a bit much.) We were on the eighteenth floor of one of the older hotels, and did it ever sway! The PA system made an urgent announcement entirely in static. We threw on some clothes and huddled together in the corridor, not knowing what to do. The PA continued it's staticky announcements—in fact, *that's* what woke my twin grandchildren, not the quake. From every room, static. Needless to say you couldn't get through to hotel information. Should we try to make our way down the eighteen floors with two octogenarians and two sixteen-month-olds?

After about ten minutes of confusion and lots of cell-phone calls to friends in LA, two security guards came by to tell us everything was okay. We could go back to our rooms. I'm grateful for sleeping potions, or there would have been no sleep for me that night.

Everyone in our party was annoyed by the nonfunctioning PA system, but their attitude was, What can you expect in Las Vegas? I was the only one to speak up. The front desk put me through to the assistant manager, who was courtly and apologetic. They'd received other calls, he conceded. They were working on it. He'd be happy to buy our party lunch.

I was too annoyed to be bought off by lunch. I asked to speak to the manager. He was gruff and rough and put me in mind of movies I'd seen about the Mob. He said they couldn't control earthquakes and repeated the offer to buy us lunch. I refused. I was certain the hotel had known about the broken PA system, hadn't bothered to fix it, wouldn't fix it now. Why should they? The hotel was filled with oblivious people proffering their money up at the tables. I invoked one of my own rules and folded.

We should have left in protest, but I gulped down my anger. I didn't want to be the one to spoil the celebration——or my kneecaps. My husband says I should have taken the lunch.

SO:

- Don't make excuses for or rationalize unacceptable treatment.
- You deserve to be compensated for unacceptable treatment.
- Know when to fold.

Expiration Date

I have a minor but annoying eye condition which I treat with nonprescription, saline drops. A half-ounce bottle of this salty water costs $16.

(I had to try four or five kinds of artificial tears before I found a concoction that worked. And buying tears is no inexpensive matter. Each bottle cost at least $8. Until I found one that worked, *I returned every bottle for a refund.*)

During a trip to France, something unfortunate happened. Toward the end of the trip, I finished one bottle of drops and opened another that I'd bought just before we left. These new drops seemed weaker and didn't do the job. My eyes started to bother me. I looked at the bottle and realized what the problem was. The drops were expired by over a *year*. The stuff had gone stale.

We'd have to find a pharmacy—in *France*—*on a Sunday.*

It was raining and we got soaked going from pharmacy to pharmacy in the city of Montpellier, but the solution was unavailable and we could find nothing comparable. This was extremely worrisome. Without the drops, I'd suffer burning eyes and blurred vision.

Lucky for me, my husband is a scientist. Guessing that the salt in the drops had crystalized, he shook the bottle and warmed it in his hand. That helped.

If this problem had arisen earlier in the trip, I would have phoned the pharmacy and asked them to airship me a fresh bottle. As it was, I had some discomfort, and a wasted afternoon hunting for a replacement.

If I'd been injured instead of inconvenienced, I would have gone to a lawyer. However, I wanted the pharmacy to compensate me for my inconvenience and their negligence. (And maybe it was worse than *mere* negligence. Another pharmacy chain was under indictment for selling expired *prescription* drugs.) How much compensation was I entitled to? I didn't know. I didn't even know what ballpark I was in.

When we got home, I told my pharmacist friend the story. He said that what had happened was very serious. I was lucky, he said, that this was only a topical solution and hadn't injured me. The next person could be in real trouble if the pharmacy didn't shape up its act. I shouldn't let the pharmacy off the hook, he advised. I should bring home to them, in monetary terms, the seriousness of their negligence. Perhaps it would be a wake-up call. Tell them, he said, that merely replacing the solution was not satisfactory—and that the FDA would like to know about the situation.

I did what he suggested, went to the store and spoke with the manager, who said he'd replace the defective drops and have someone from the company's headquarters call me. The strange thing was, when the manager examined the bottle of expired solution, he looked puzzled.

"I don't understand," he said. "We don't even carry the 2-percent solution, we only carry the five." I *believe* he was being honest, that's the scary part. He certainly wasn't challenging me because *his* store's label was on the box. Did this huge chain have *any* track of its inventory?

The next day I got a call from a woman identifying herself as head of "Risk Management." The name says it all. Today, large corporations have Risk Management departments—an admission, it seems to me, that they make mistakes so often they need an entire division to protect them, to "manage" the consequences of their screw-ups. (I was amazed they didn't give it a more euphemistic name.)

Ms. Risk Management tried to manage me. She offered me $400 for my trouble. "That's all I can offer you," she said—with conviction. I almost accepted. I was grateful for any offer at all. But then I remembered that a first offer is just that, a *first* offer, no matter how final she sounded.

"Let me speak with your supervisor," I said.

"I have no supervisor," she said. "I'm the *only* one who can make this offer." Gulp. She was God. There was no one above her. Her tactic almost worked.

"I'll think about it," I said.

When I got off the phone, my husband said, "Take the $400. It's not worth your time writing letters."

The voice in my head repeated over and over—*a first offer is just a first offer.*

"One more call," I said, "then I'll let it go."

The next morning I called and told her I understood she was the head of the department, but even so, I wanted to talk with *her* boss, whoever that might be. Then I played good-guy, bad-guy. I cast myself as the good guy, and my husband as the bad guy.

"The $400 is all right with me," I said, "but my husband's very upset. He expected us to get a thousand. He's talking about going to his attorney." (He doesn't have an attorney.)

"I can go as high as $600," she said.

Here's a glaring example of business *not* behaving in an honorable manner. The woman lied to me—is there any other word for it? She'd said she couldn't go higher than $400. When I challenged her, she maintained the lie. And I'm sure if I called her the *following* day, the offer would have been even higher, but I felt $600 was adequate.

My husband, at the breakfast table, was eating crow when I hung up the phone.

The next time I bought the drops, I checked the expiration date, which was fine, but guess what? They tried to sell me a bottle of the 2-percent solution again—which the manager claimed they never carry. Scarey. Certainly it's buyer beware.

When I told my friend Sharon about the incident, she gasped. Something similar had happened to her, except with a *prescription* drug. She'd ordered a refill of Prempro, a hormone replacement, but had been given, instead, Provocal, a statin for lowering cholesterol.

When she called the pharmacy and told them about their error, they apologized abjectly. Evidently, they'd given Sharon's prescription to someone else. They offered to deliver the correct prescription immediately, and Sharon said okay. She let the pharmacy off the hook for what could have been a dangerous, possibly a fatal, error. What's especially troubling about this mistake is that statins are generally used by older people who might not notice the difference, and they *must* be taken daily. But Sharon felt satisfied with the way she'd handled the situation—until she heard *my* story, and then she had second thoughts.

What happened here was that Sharon confused behavior appropriate in a friendship with behavior appropriate for transacting business. If a friend makes a mistake, you accept their apology and continue the friendship. You might discuss the incident and ask for some modification of the friend's behavior. No restitution is required. When a business makes an egregious error—an error that could cause serious harm, they should be held accountable and given some incentive to correct their faulty system.

SO:

- Merely replacement of a product that inconvenienced you is not enough. You can ask to be compensated for your inconvenience. Businesses should be held accountable for their negligence.
- Rack your brains for someone in your life who's an expert in the area and get advice before you present your problem to the perpetrator.
- A first offer is only that, a *first* offer. Don't immediately accept it because you're so grateful to get *any* offer. If you ask them to go higher, they usually will.
- And very important, don't forget, dealing with business is not the same as dealing with friends. Our entire society is confused about how to interface with business.

11.

Asking to Be Treated Fairly

There are some situations where we're simply asking to be treated fairly, asking for a business or an institution to make good on their original promise, to follow through on their commitments.

Pst, Have I Got a Deal for You

Always check your sales slip at the supermarket. Sometimes this week's specials don't make it into the computer. Or it can be more devious than that. Some supermarket and drug chains are under indictment for routinely setting the prices in their computers higher than those advertised on the shelf. *Consumer Reports* cites a study by the Federal Trade Commission and the U.S. Department of Commerce, which found that at "23 percent of the stores, more than 2 percent of the items scanned incorrectly."[1] If you're overcharged for an item, the store will usually give it to you for free. But you might have to remind them of this policy.

In a three-for sale—buy three and get a special price—you don't have to actually buy three to get the price. The store just wants you to think that. Buy one and get the discount.[2]

SO:

- Check your sales slip and ask to get the item free if you've been overcharged.

Buy Now, Save Later

It used to be that when you sent off a rebate offer, you could put it out of your mind with the confidence that, in due time—maybe a *long* time—you'd receive the promised rebate. Things have changed. In recent years, high-stake rebate offers have become a staple of the computer market. Anywhere from $10 to $100 rebates are offered. But sometimes—actually too many times—the rebate checks never show up.

That's what happened to me three times in a year, all involving a major computer retailer that cosponsors offers with computer companies. A $10 rebate on a mouse, a $30 rebate on software, a $20 rebate on a box of floppys, never materialized—and I had *not* made copies of the receipts.

I called the retailer and explained I hadn't received my rebates. After "researching" my purchases for twenty minutes, they rebated me my money. Luckily, I was able to use my credit card statements as proof of my purchases, but the process would have been easier if I'd kept copies of the actual receipts, the rebate coupons, and the proofs of purchase. These days, I keep copies of paperwork on anything over $5.

And I *never* received the rebates in the mail—which makes you wonder.

Another rebate failure is when the merchant doesn't bother to remove displays of expired rebate coupons, and you buy an item thinking you'll get a rebate. That happened to me at Staples. I bought a toner cartridge with a $15 rebate only to discover later that the coupon had expired a month before. I called the store and the manager said to bring in the coupon and my receipt and he would give me the $15.

SO:

- Keep copies of paperwork on a rebate offer.
- If you purchased an item with the understanding that you would receive a rebate and the rebate offer has expired, ask the merchant to make good on his mistake.

A Moving Experience

Moving companies. This is an area where you can't win—but you can minimize your losses. It will always be bad, it's just a question of how bad.

When I moved cross-country, I decided to use a national mover even though I was quoted lower prices by independent movers. At least I'd have some leverage when they screwed up—as they inevitably would.

First of all, movers are always late. One to two hours. Are they really coming? you wonder. You call. They're on their way, the dispatcher tells you. Another half hour goes by. Yes, they're on their way. Should be there soon. And for cross-country moves, count on them not arriving at your new home when they say they will, by *days,* not hours.

Harriett was driving cross-country with me. We'd heard the stories about movers being late, so we decided to pack air mattresses and camp out in my apartment in San Diego. But when the van driver saw us carrying the mattresses to the car, he said it wouldn't be necessary. He'd arrive when promised, he assured us. He was definitive, and we were easily persuaded. More room for tapes, clothes, and anything we bought along the way.

Large movers have satellite dishes on their vans enabling headquarters to pinpoint their location at any time. We called the 800 number and checked on our van the first few days. All was on schedule. We could have a relaxing drive and stop at all the places we wanted to see—except the Grand Canyon. We wouldn't have time to make the two-day detour.

On the last night of our trip, in Yuma, Arizona, we called to make sure the movers were on track. What we learned, shocked us. The driver had arrived in California ahead of schedule, and had already left for Arkansas to pick up another California shipment. He'd be two days late. With all their sophisticated equipment, no one had bothered to reach us. We'd already missed the Grand Canyon, and now we'd arrive two days ahead of the truck—without air mattresses. We should have called every day, but we'd grown complacent.

Tired of staying in motels, we bought more air mattresses, bedding, shower curtain, towels. The bill came to $135. I asked the company to reimburse me—at the very least—but this was not one of my great successes. They only reimbursed me half. The driver "shouldn't have advised us not to take the camping equipment," they said. Their tone implied he *hadn't.*

When I told the driver how disappointed I was by his inconsideration, that he'd prevented us from seeing the Grand Canyon, he shrugged. He'd seen the Grand Canyon, he said, and, "it wasn't really that much." (Don't use movers for tour guides.)

On the insurance question, I've gone both ways—bought insurance, not bought it—with the same results. Stuff gets damaged, they'll generally fix it if you persist.

SO:

- ✦ When moving, expect aggravation. That's the norm.
- ✦ Call the 800 number *every day* no matter what assurances they give you. Stay on top of it.
- ✦ Use a large mover for cross-country moves. That way you'll have *some* recourse.

You Be the Judge

I received an offer for a Macy's Premier Visa Card. The benefits of the card included 3 percent off Macy's purchases, 1 percent off other purchases, "double reward" events, and "periodic" $25-dollar Reward Certificates. All this and no annual fee. It sounded like a good deal to me.

I filled out the form and sent if off. A few weeks later my Premier card arrived. Since I don't buy much at Macy's, I forgot about the card until one day, a few months later, I realized I hadn't received any perks—no bonuses, no rebates, nothing. I pulled out my wallet and looked at the card. It wasn't a Premier **Visa** card. It was just a Premier card. I searched through my papers and found a copy of the original offer. It was for a Premier **Visa.** Premier, Premier Visa. Too close for comfort. Not only hadn't I received benefits from the "Premier" card, but because I'd used it instead of my Citibank Visa, I had forgone frequent-flier miles.

I expressed my distress to an assistant manager. She apologized for the mix-up. There must have been some kind of mistake. "Human error," was how she put it. I could bring in my receipts, and they would credit them back to my account and then charge them on my Citibank card and get the frequent-flier miles. That was too much work, I said. Macy's needed to come up with a better way of retaining my business. The woman immediately offered me a $50 gift certificate for my trouble.

You be the judge. How many others have received Premier cards rather than Premier Visa cards and not noticed?

SO:

- ＋ Businesses engage in confusing practices.
- ＋ Periodically check to see if you're receiving what was promised.
- ＋ Ask to be compensated for misleading information that causes you to lose money.

You Can't Bank On It

Banks are another area where assumptions can cause trouble. I grew up believing that banks don't make mistakes. And judging by the fact that most people don't balance their checkbooks—you're accused of being anal if you do—this is a pretty widely held belief. But banks aren't what they used to be, or what we *thought* they were. They *do* make mistakes—big ones.

I received a check for a matured CD that was $1,014.14 less than it should have been.

"Yes," the clerk said, when I called the bank. "Thirty-one percent was sent to the IRS because you never completed a W9."

"But, but, but," I sputtered, "I signed everything you sent me." The clerk was definitive. No, I hadn't signed it; therefore the money was sent to the IRS for withholding.

I was almost intimidated into accepting the unacceptable. I *had* moved during the past year. It *was* possible the form had gotten lost in the mail. Still, I saw no reason why I couldn't fill out the form now and get my money.

"There's nothing we can do," she said. "The file is closed, and the money sent to the IRS."

"Let me talk to a supervisor," I said.

"Just one moment, but it won't do you any good. The IRS has the money." My face got hot, my stomach growled.

"Miss Rollin," the supervisor said, "Can you please hold while we find your file?" My actual file, real papers?

She was apologetic when she returned to the line. "We *do* have a signed W9 in your file. We'll send you a check for the withheld amount."

"Plus interest," I said. "You've had the money for twenty days."

"All right, we'll send you a check for the interest."

A few days later, I received a check for the $1,014.14, and a few days after that, another one for $67, which I calculated to be twenty days of interest for the *entire* amount of the CD, not just the $1,014.14. Who was doing their numbers?

A week after that, I received *another* piece of mail from them. What now? Our business was finished. I would never invest with them again. I was ready to throw the letter away, but a morbid curiosity made my fingers slit the envelope open.

It contained one sheet of paper that looked similar to the notice of maturity I'd originally received. My eyes fell on the number, $1,014.14, then on the words, **"Renewal Notice."** They'd sent me a renewal notice for a CD of $1,014 maturing in thirty months. I had no more money with them. How messed up was *this* institution? (My husband remarked that the 5.34 percent interest rate was rather low.)

In thirty months, *this* bank will probably have been taken over by the FDIC, but it'll be interesting to see what happens. Will they catch the error?

SO:

+ Banks make mistakes.
+ Don't be intimidated into accepting the unacceptable.
+ Persist.
+ Ask for interest when a bank hangs onto your money longer than you've authorized them to.

Another Scary Bank Story

Banks aren't what they used to be, especially when they merge. One institution I had an account with merged with another. During the transition, they supposedly lost track of the maturity dates of CDs and were automatically renewing them—*without* sending out expiration notices—at a very low rate. It took many phone calls and faxes to cash in a recently matured CD. Not only didn't they apologize for their "error," but an employee practically begged me to renew my CD with them. The whole thing smelled as fishy as hell.

You *can't* bank on it. Check everything.

SO:

- Problems arise when banks merge. Don't rely on them to do *anything* right.
- Check everything.

Promises, Promises

It's been in the news that banks are slipping in all kinds of little fees that are almost below the awareness level. You have to check your statements carefully.

When my husband and I opened a joint checking account, we were promised there'd be no fees. No fees for copies of checks, no fees for overdraft protection, no fees for the ATM card. But on our first statement, all three fees appeared for a total of $4.50. When I showed the error to the bank manager, he apologized and said he would change it in the computer.

The next month the charges appeared again. And the next. The bank manager admitted there was *no* way he could change it in the computer because, in the recent merger (there's that word again), the system had been reconfigured to *automatically add these fees to everyone's account*. He apologized and credited us with a year's fees, promising to do the same next year. For those who Ask.

SO:

- Banks try to slip in fees.
- Persistence will get these fees dropped.
- Bank tellers have *some* discretion.

Reversal of Fortune

This story is about buying that dream house and having it turn into a nightmare experience. When we were house hunting, the market was booming and prices were zooming. After eight months of searching, and some false starts, we finally found the right house. Nice and light, not too big, quiet. We were the first to see it and we jumped on it, made the sellers a fair offer, which they accepted. That turned out to be the easy part. The next hurdle was getting a mortgage.

Naturally, we wanted the best rate and terms. We searched the newspaper, the Internet, we called. It was all so confusing. I'd been in real estate for fifteen years, but I wasn't prepared for what we went through. First of all, we needed to lock in a rate quickly because interest rates were rising. Being out of the loop now, I felt as frustrated and confused as any buyer. Points, no points. Three-year loans, ten-year loans, seven-year loans. And there was no consistency in the way rates and terms were quoted. Most difficult of all was finding out the lender's fees. Each one we spoke to had a different way of describing their charges—and they all sounded put out that we would even ask. It wasn't as if we were being hairsplitters. These costs ranged from $700 to $2,000. Trying to find out the hidden costs was as slippery as catching fish with your bare hands.

The real estate agent recommended a mortgage broker. A mortgage broker is someone who "brokers" loans to various institutions. They get their fees from the institution—and whatever they can get out of you. They can be useful in that *they* can shop around for the lowest rate, but you have to be careful about the hidden costs. This mortgage broker sounded sincere.

"I can get you the lowest possible rates," she promised.

As to what *her* costs were, she rapid-fired off a list of charges in the same annoyed tone the others had used—I had to speed write them down. They totaled about $1,000, which seemed reasonable for obtaining the "lowest" rates. We made an appointment for an application the following day.

Just before leaving the house, my husband received a call from the assisted-living facility where his parents lived. His ninety-year-old father had fallen and broken his hip. We'd have to speed up the loan application and rush to the hospital, but the application took longer than it should have because the broker was juggling two applications simultaneously. She kept rushing back and forth between offices.

In between her flights, we tried to pin her down on rates and terms, but we couldn't get a straight answer on anything. A simple question like, what are today's rates? inspired the reading of an article about the long bond. We sat there baffled. And what are her charges? She pulled out a form and filled in some blanks. The charges were the same as the ones she'd quoted on the phone, but there was an additional miscellaneous charge of $200.

"What's this extra $200?" I asked.

"Oh, I put that in," she said by way of nonexplanation.

Then we learned that she would lock-in our rate for only

fifteen days. What good was a fifteen-day lock when it took thirty days to close escrow? We assumed thirty-day locks were customary, we told her. She looked at us as if we were nuts.

"Nobody gives thirty-day locks," she said, "but if that's what you want, it will cost you an extra point." (If you haven't bought a house recently, a point is 1 percent of the mortgage amount— in our case, $2,400.) Maybe *I* was crazy—and she half-had me believing it—but I could swear the other lenders had thirty-day locks.

In the middle of all this confusion, she said there was something I *must* see and practically dragged me into another office to show me pictures of her granddaughter. This woman kept pretending to be a real human being, but I wasn't fooled.

Finally, when we saw that we'd *never* get finished, we left without signing and rushed off to the hospital.

That night, we sat across the dinner table and compared notes. The woman hadn't given us one straight answer. If she wants to do business with us, we decided, she'll have to tell us the rate, give us a thirty-day lock, and put her costs in writing.

But my stomach turned over in revulsion. To think we'd have to deal with this slimer for thirty days. And I knew her kind. We might be successful in pinning her down tomorrow, but the next day, she'd slip in something else.

"Let's fire her," I said. "It never works out doing business with the devil."

And fire her we did early the next morning, without explanation. "We've decided not to do business with you," I said.

"Can I ask you why?" she asked.

"No," I said, "I don't care to discuss it."

This was one time I trusted my gut. We were even willing to pay more *not* to deal with her. But we'd never *know* if we paid more since we couldn't get an honest quote out of her.

So back to the Internet. Banks this time—no middle man. Bank of America was offering an excellent rate and actually disclosed their exact costs. Also, a thirty-day lock *was* standard as it was with the other lenders we spoke with. They took our application over the phone and we were approved in an hour. What a difference! But here comes a David and Goliath story if ever there was one. And all we were asking for was to be treated fairly.

Since the new home was a condominium, scads of documents clogged our mailbox immediately. I waded through them as best I could, paying attention to budgets and minutes of recent meetings. There was one item, an "action" against the developer that, during our escrow, turned into a lawsuit. It seemed that the developer had planted trees with invasive roots in a green area, and the roots were interfering with the functioning of an artificial stream.

From my experience in real estate, I knew that it was common for condominium associations to sue developers for any unsettled matters, large or small, before the ten-year statute of limitations was up. And this seemed of small concern as our house wasn't anywhere near the green area, which, in fact, was quite beautiful even without the flowing water.

Our appraiser felt differently. Although he appraised the house at full price, he wrote on the appraisal that he couldn't guarantee that the lawsuit wouldn't influence future values. He also said that "kitchen sinks and slabs" might be affected. He got all this information from another realtor who had had a deal fall through, *supposedly* because of the lawsuit. It sounded nuts. Our house was nowhere near the troubled area and even over there, no houses were being lifted off the ground by gigunda roots.

This all happened three days before closing. The Bank of America people now sounded iffy.

"We don't like to hear the word 'slab,'" the underwriter told us.

We were stunned. Throughout the escrow, Bank of America had assured us that there were no problems. We'd given notice on our apartment, hired movers, packed our stuff, changed phone numbers, addresses. Everything.

We were very confused. On the one hand, I remembered from my days as a realtor that appraisers can be capricious and sometimes just plain stupid. I'd seen them kill deals out of ignorance. Still, if the bank was concerned about slabs, maybe we should be, too. Maybe we were well out of the deal. Maybe prices would drop in the community. But this made no sense. Houses were selling in forty-eight hours and other lenders were making loans.

I asked the underwriter to call the lawyers who represented the condo association and get the real story from them. She said she would, but the next morning, she called to say that the bank had "declined" to make the loan.

"What did the lawyers say?" I asked her.

"Oh, I didn't call them."

"You didn't? Why not?"

"I decided not to." Just like that. Deny us a home we badly wanted without having the decency to thoroughly examine the situation. That was Friday.

We spent the weekend hashing things over. Why hadn't the underwriter called the lawyers? It seemed to us she'd rather casually dropped the ball and dropped us on our heads. She forgot, as businesses often do, that she was dealing with real live people.

Meanwhile, our realtor was frantically scurrying around trying to find out about the other sale that had fallen through. What she learned was that the dead deal had resulted from a lawsuit involving *another* condominium complex nearby. It had *nothing* to do with our section.

Monday morning I called the underwriter, told her what the realtor had learned, and asked her to call the lawyers—*as she had promised*. I pointed out that there were *two thousand* homes in our section. If Bank of America turned down our loan, they would lose this huge market.

The underwriter said she'd get her Legal Department to call the condo association's lawyers. Two hours later, she called back. Did we still want the house?

"Only if *you* can assure us there's nothing wrong," I said.

"The lawyers explained it to us," she said. "It's not very significant. It's just regarding the plantings in the common area. They expect a settlement from the developer soon. We'll get the appraiser to redo the appraisal." I wonder how they did *that*. Aren't appraisers supposed to be neutral and independent? "We'll fax you the papers, and you can close in two days."

Along with the closing papers, was a handwritten apology. In between relief and packing, my husband and I tried to sort out what had happened. Why had the bank reversed itself—a definite "No" on Friday to an unconditional "Yes" on Monday? What we concluded was that the underwriter had, at first, taken the path of least resistance; she smelled a little trouble and fled—a combination of incompetence and laziness. Too much trouble to call the lawyers; turn down the loan.

She needed to be reminded that they were dealing with human beings. She needed to be held to her word that she'd promised to call the lawyers.

My husband says what happened is I turned a bank into a person.

(Incidentally, the value of our house has gone up 20 percent since we bought it nine months ago, and no unwanted roots have crossed the threshold.)

SO:

- ✦ Make sure you get all the fees itemized in writing.
- ✦ Trust your gut. Don't do business (or anything else) with a person or institution when it doesn't feel right for whatever reason.
- ✦ Don't let business off the hook. If they promised to do something, hold their feet to the fire.
- ✦ If something doesn't sound right, don't let it go by. Ask questions, persist, persist, persist.

12.

Asking for
the Information You Need

Asking can be simply asking for the information you need to make a decision. But information can be hard to come by. It can take a lot of time, thereby inconveniencing others while you are pursuing it, and it can be difficult to find—you have to wade through layers of bureaucracy to get to it. The following stories are of situations where getting information saved a lot of trouble "down the road."

Location, Location, Location

Information was what we needed the first time we found the "perfect house." Perfect except for one thing. The house was on a wide, beautiful, quiet boulevard—that part was great—except the boulevard ended abruptly a half a block from the house, the end marked by a flimsy wooden fence. Behind the fence was vacant land, lots of it. The boulevard wanted to go somewhere and the little fence wasn't going to hold it back.

"Is there a plan for the road?" I asked the realtor.

She waved her hand dismissively. "Oh, sometime in the future they'll probably extend it to the freeway." It sounded as if we were talking about twenty-five years or so. My husband shuffled impatiently, or at least I imagined he did. He was delighted with the house. Our hunt was over. We could get out of our cramped, little apartment. I almost dropped the subject of the road. I *almost* didn't ask.

"Could you find out? Maybe the listing agent will know." (If the town of Antioch, near San Francisco, has it's way, realtors will have to disclose traffic congestion.)[1]

The realtor called to say that the road *would* be linked up to the Interstate, but an environmental group was delaying it because the area was a nesting site for the endangered gnat-catcher.

Suddenly, things sounded more immediate. We had intended to write an offer that night, but I suggested we wait and call Planning and Zoning.

"What do you expect to find out?" my husband asked. (I'm pretty sure he sounded annoyed.)

"I don't know, maybe we'll hear that it's in the twenty-five-year plan or that the environmentalists are successfully blocking it." That's what I *hoped* anyway.

It took about ten calls to get through to the right department. Then some kind soul connected me with the project engineer. He gave me the no-nonsense story on the road. Good news for commuters; bad news for us.

"The plans call for widening the road to six lanes and extending it to the Interstate and beyond."

Gulp.

"When will the work start?" From my years in real estate, I knew that "plans" were often just that, plans. In the Washington, D.C., area, there was a "plan" for an outer beltway. This plan had been talked about for fifteen years. No dirt had been moved yet.

Different story here. "The plans have been approved and the money allocated. Work is scheduled to start within a few months. The road," he continued, "will be a prime arterial."

A prime arterial. What's a prime arterial? He used the term as if I would know what it meant. I had to force myself to "ask" and risk sounding like an idiot.

"What's a prime arterial?"

"A prime arterial? Oh, that's, well . . . one step down from a freeway."

"So . . . that doesn't sound like a great street to buy a house on?"

"Probably not." He chuckled. "My sister almost bought a house there but decided not to."

And I'd come close to *not* asking.

This is one of the difficulties in asking—you risk embarrassing or irritating others. Sometimes I've not asked or half-asked because I was afraid of being annoying. But there's a big difference between refraining from sending a dish back and getting critical information for an important decision. You *have* to risk being annoying.

This situation reminds me of something that happened thirty years ago, *before* I'd thought much about asking. My parents took me and my great-aunt, a world traveler and a self-acknowledged gourmet, to dinner at a new restaurant that served, of all things, British fare. This was quite a novelty. In fact, it may have been the first—and **the last**—British restaurant on Long Island. (What were we thinking? British *food!*) The John Peel Room, it was called.

The restaurant was clubby and horsey—leather banquets with brass tacking, framed hunting scenes, dim lighting. Not only were the menus hard to read, but the dishes were puzzling.

My parents and I still share a mortified laugh remembering that night.

My mother, normally the Ultimate in unabashed asking, carefully perused the menu. One of the appetizers was called Melton Mowbry. No description.

"What's Melton Mowbry?" my mother asked the waiter, who was outfitted as an English groom. When he spoke, though, we knew he was a fellow New Yorker from the borough of Brooklyn.

He humphed impatiently—as if any idiot would know Melton Mowbry. "It's Melton," he said, "with a Mowbry sauce."

My aunt, the world traveler, my parents, savvy New York-ers, and me in a preask state, said, in unison, "Oh," and went back to the business of studying the menu.

We still don't know what Melton Mowbry is. No one had the guts to order it.

SO:

- If you have an unresolved issue, risk annoying the other people involved to pursue it.
- Purchasing a house is perhaps the largest single purchase you'll make in a lifetime. Ask with abandon.
- Determination helps. Decide that you *will* be able to find the information you need. It may take many phone calls, but if it's important, do it.
- Don't let waiters intimidate you.

Rent and Repent

Car rentals is another area where you need information to make a decision—and, in this case too, information isn't easy to come by. The quoted price seldom includes all the extra charges, which vary from company to company and location to location. Sometimes even the booking agent doesn't know all of the charges. You'll need to press on to get the total costs.

First the good news. As with hotels, car rental agencies give discounts. You just have to ask. AAA, AARP, corporate. Anywhere from 10 to 15 percent for barely mentioning it. What this means is that the *real* price is 10 to 15 percent lower than the advertised price. Also, they sometimes run specials, but you need to ask.

Now for the down side. Remember my friends, Sharon and Lucy, who were shocked at the final cost of their rental car? There's a good reason for that. This is one of the more murky, confusing areas of consumerism, and unfortunately, we have to deal with it when we're in a rush—usually when we've just arrived in a strange city. There are so many twists and turns in the quagmire of car renting that you probably should take an attorney with you or at least an armed guard. Charges fly at you like free radicals. Often they're not disclosed till your final bill. Unless you ask.

When you call a rental agency, ask for a complete list of charges—*everything* included. Bizarre things are slipped in like "airport recovery fees," an extra 10 percent that Hertz tags on at the Jacksonville airport. Now, I admit that a recovered airport would make a nifty souvenir, but I wasn't aware I had *lost* an airport. As to additional insurance, which they try to push on you, most people are covered by their MasterCards, Visas, or their car insurance. Check before you leave home. Purchasing the rental agency's insurance is usually a total waste.

I called Hertz and Enterprise for quotes on the same itinerary. In both cases I had to ask for the total charges—they weren't volunteered—and they were considerable. Enterprise charges an "airport access fee" of 6 percent. Supposedly it's to pay for their being located on airport property. (I think I'd rather pay the 10 percent and *recover* the airport.) Enterprise also tags on a $2-a-day "surcharge." Surcharge for what? The privilege of doing business with them? What this means is that the car *actually* costs an additional $2 a day. Neither the "airport access fee" nor the "surcharge" were mentioned when they quoted the rates. I had to ask.

And don't make the mistake of assuming that extra days will be prorated on the weekly rate. Enterprise quoted me $196.95 for a week, which comes to $28.14 a day—very reasonable for a full-size car. Extra days, I found out *when I asked,* are $41.45! And there is no standard policy on this. Some rental agencies *will* prorate, and even if their initial rates are higher, the total might come to less. In fact, there's no standard policy on *anything,* even within a company. Different sites have different policies.

And there's no standard return policy. Enterprise has a fifty-nine-minute leeway before you're charged extra. That means, if you pick the car up at noon on Monday, you'll be charged for only one day if you return it by 12:59 P.M. on Tuesday. If you return it at 1:00, you'll be charged an extra quarter of the daily rate. I assumed that meant that the day was divided into quarters and for every six hours, you paid $10.36, but actually, you get charged a quarter of the daily rate for every *hour* you're late. Kind of a lot for a car you thought cost $28.14 a day.

Hertz has a one-hour grace period—one more minute than Enterprise. Extra days were $41, the same as Enterprise.

"What happens after the grace period?" I asked.

"It *should* be a charge of about one-third of a day for each hour. But if you're three hours and one minute over, you get charged for the entire additional day."

"What do you mean 'should be'?" I asked. "Don't you know?"

"I can't guarantee anything that's going to happen in the computer. *You* know," she said, "it's the way car rentals are." So I was learning.

In addition to state taxes, Hertz tags on a rental surcharge of $2.03 a day—for "highway maintenance." Then there's a 35-cent-a-day "vehicle license fee recovery." So now I'm not only recovering an airport, I'm recovering a license. Whose license? Yours, mine, Hertz's? It was, I was told, "the proportionate amount of the vehicle licensing fee that Hertz is allowed to collect from the customer." Talk about needing a lawyer.

Also, she told me that "an assessment of our driving records may be a condition of the rental." I'd never heard that before. And there'd be a $5 charge per day for an additional driver unless we each had our own AAA accounts. I'd thought it was universally accepted that married people didn't pay extra. That policy is also variable. In fact, if you're traveling with a friend, you might be assessed anywhere from $3 to $5 a day for an additional driver. Since I've kept my own name, I probably need to carry a copy of our marriage license to prove we're married!

And drop-off fees. What will it cost to drop the car off at another location?

By the way, if you make the slightest change on your reservation prior to your trip, the initial rate may "cancel out" and you'll get charged the current rate. Usually, that's not good news.

Sounds complicated? It doesn't have to be. You can just close your eyes and sign, making sure to take out a second mortgage first. Or, if you don't have the time (or patience) to check on all the extra charges when you make the reservation, when you get home, call and insist you were never informed of them. The charges will be dropped without hassle. They *know* you were never informed.

Whoops! Something else. The gas policy. Usually, the least costly thing to do is return a car with a full tank. Some rental agencies will quote you a low price per gallon if you don't have a full tank, but what they forget to mention is that you'll pay for a *whole* tank if the needle isn't on full.

Sound too complicated? Maybe a check list will help. When you rent a car, here's what you need to find out:

- Whether your credit card or your car insurance covers the rental
- The weekly rate
- The daily rate
- The return policy
- The alternate drop-off fee
- Any surcharges
- Taxes
- Additional driver fee

- Gas policy
- Discount
- Return-time leeway
- Bonus frequent-flier miles

SO:

- It's easy to get discounts on car rentals.
- Rent ahead of time and use the checklist.
- Be on the lookout for off-the-wall charges.

13.

Doing Graduate Work

Graduate work involves situations that begin with a simple Ask but then grow more complex and challenging. You've worked your way up to this point **and you can handle it. These are the daring, outrageous acts of Ask.** They're complex and take a lot of persistence and nerve.

These are Asks that most people would be too intimidated to try. To use circus terms, they're colossal, stupendous feats of daring, except they're accomplished with words not actions. It took years for me to reach the point where I was courageous enough to attempt some of the Asks in this section. If you can build on my accomplishments, it might only take you months. Soon, you may be willing to try some feats of daring yourself.

You Wouldn't Dare, or, Some Nerve

The following two stories are examples of asking that are far more outrageous than most people would try, or even approve of. See what you think.

An apartment I was about to rent had been carpeted by the vacating tenant with inexpensive, too-green carpeting. He offered to sell it to me for $600. I didn't think it was worth it, so I said no, even though tenants were required to keep 80 percent of the floor carpeted. I gambled that the tenant might leave it anyway——which he did.

I asked the management who owned the carpet now? It was mine, they told me. I had them write this into the lease.

Now here's the outrageous part. When I was getting ready to move, the new tenant admired the carpet. Would I sell it to him? I sold it to him for $300.

The second incident happened while I was living in the same building. One day a young couple stopped me just as I was entering the lobby. Did I live here? they asked. Did I like it? They were new in town and hunting for an apartment. I chatted with them and answered their questions, then I asked: "Could you tell the rental office I sent you? They pay a referral fee."

"Sure," they said.

And sure enough, they rented an apartment and I was paid a $350 referral fee. But I had to ask for it, nobody volunteered.

SO:

• There's nothing too outrageous to ask for.

Dismemberment

We've *all* joined a gym and felt guilty about not using it while we paid the monthly fee. I did it again this year and suffered buyer's remorse almost immediately. I'd never be able to get myself across that huge pool or discipline myself to use those machines.

A sleepless night followed. The only thing I had going for me was that this gym was part of the Jewish Community Center, a nonprofit organization. I called the membership guy the next morning and told him I'd made a mistake; membership wasn't for me, was all I said.

"No problem," he said, "we'll credit your Visa." Thus I was easily able to resume my sloth.

In many states there's a three-day right-of-recision for gym contracts.

Even if you keep a membership though, if your situation changes, you can ask for some leeway in the "rules." One winter my daughter signed up for a year's membership in a fitness center; but when summer came, she realized that she preferred getting her exercise outdoors. She asked the gym to suspend her membership for the summer months. They'd do it, they said, for a fee. So she asked them to waive the fee and they did.

SO:

- You don't have to be stuck with a mistake you made; ask to have it remedied.
- When the urge to exercise arises, beat it down. It might lead to joining a gym.

To Cell or Not to Cell

Cell phones have rapidly become ubiquitous, and the dizzying array of pricing plans is enough to make you nuts. My daughter's friend Trisha was on a family reunion at a remote campground in the northwest when she learned from the kennel that her dog was ill. The only way to reach the outside world from the campground was by cell phone, and Trisha ran up quite a bill, far exceeding the allowable calls on her calling plan. The dog recovered, but when Trisha got her cell-phone bill, she freaked. Instead of a bill of $29.99 for 150 local minutes, her bill was $290, $220 of it in roaming charges. She called my daughter and asked her what to do. "Ask," was what my daughter advised. Trisha called her cell-phone carrier, AT&T Wireless and learned that once a year, they will adjust your calling plan retroactively for just such a situation. AT&T allowed her to retroactively switch to the Digital One Rate plan at the monthly rate of $59.99. With this rate she received three hundred minutes a month with no long distance or roaming charges. AT&T also allows you to call ahead and switch your plan one month at a time, if you foresee your usage will be different from usual.

I had the same thing happen to me that month. A family crisis made me far exceed my one hundred anywhere minutes for $29.99 a month. I called my carrier, Verizon, and asked for help. They, too, will adjust a bill in the same way, once a year, "as a courtesy" (translation, for those who ask). But Verizon stipulated that you have to remain on the adjusted plan for two months, which would not have netted me much of a savings.

"That won't help me much, having to pay $55 a month for two months, instead of $29.99," I said.

"All right," the operator said, "just this once we can waive that policy, but we can't keep doing that."

Verizon says they won't allow you to change your calling plan more than once a year, unlike AT&T, which allows you to go on a different calling plan one month at a time. (Ask anyway).

SO:

+ Nothing is cast in stone. Charges can be adjusted retroactively. Ask.
+ If you're satisfied with one aspect of a company's offer, but not another, ask for that to be adjusted also.
+ "Just this once," "As a courtesy." These policies are *not* advertised. You will *not* find them in the brochures. They're only available to those who Ask.

Pay in Advance

Did you ever think you could get a *lawyer* to give you a refund? And pigs will grow wings and fly, right?

For help with a complicated pension issue, I was referred by a lawyer friend to a pension law expert. When I called the expert, her assistant interviewed me on the nature of my problem and said she'd get back to me. When she did, she notified me that the attorney needed $250 before she would look at my case.

I hand-delivered a check, a letter outlining my specific questions, and the relevant documents. A few days later, I received a letter from the attorney saying, in effect, that I didn't have a prayer of getting a cent in my situation because I hadn't worked the required time—a fact she knew from the information I'd given her assistant *before* she demanded $250.

I felt taken advantage of, but not knowing my rights, I called my lawyer friend. One of the principles of *Ask!*—do your homework.

He was incensed. The matter could have been handled, he thought, in a straightforward, less costly manner. So I called Ms. Money-Grabber's assistant and asked for a refund. The assistant talked to her boss and called me back immediately. They would send me a check for $125.

SO:

* Do your homework. Get as much information as you can before addressing a problem.
* You're entitled to get your money's worth on a service as well as a product.
* Even attorneys will give refunds if asked.

Museum Manqué

A few years ago I took my kids and their friends—five of us in all—to a privately run architectural exhibit by a famous architect. The tour, supposed to be an hour, was barely a half hour and run by a docent-in-training. We were disappointed and appalled at what it had cost—$15 each. The next day I called the museum office and asked for a supervisor.

"We were terribly disappointed with our tour yesterday," I said.

"Yes, we were understaffed and had to use a new docent. I'm really sorry about that." I could tell she thought the conversation ended there.

"We'd like a refund," I said.

"Oh . . . Okay. We'll credit your Visa. I have the receipt right here."

An apology is good. An apology with a refund is better.

SO:

- Again, there's nothing too outrageous to ask for. Redress is available in even the most exotic situations.

The Play's the Thing

A friend walked out of a play after the first act. The supposedly professional performance was distinctly amateurish. After reading sections of *Ask!* she wrote to the theater and asked for a refund. This is groundbreaking. I've *never* heard of anyone even asking for a refund from a theater.

She E-mailed me the results:

> *The playhouse sent me a letter of apology for the bad performance together with two free tickets for 2000 performance or I may exchange them for a 2001 performance.*

SO:

+ You can ask for *anything.* If you're dissatisfied with something, ask for a remedy.

Ignore the Fine Print

Stel and her husband, Fred, booked a Mediterranean cruise at a great price, air included. They decided to make their own flight arrangements because the cruise line's were inconvenient. They would just have to pay more. In the cruise contract, it stated clearly that there would be no refunds for unused flights. Once aboard, though, they heard about a passenger who had ignored the fine print. Stel E-mailed me the story.

> We had heard from someone on the cruise that he had his airfare rebated, even though it expressly states in the documents that they will not do this if it is part of the package. Fred called twice to check and after the second call was not returned, he got in touch with a supervisor, complained about the poor treatment, and said, not only will he not use the cruise line again, but will inform his friends as well. (Spoke nicely, but firmly, stressing the poor customer response.) She said to mail her the documentation, she'd see what she could do . . . the rest is history—a $731 credit toward another cruise. (The entire cost for the two of us was only $1800 to begin with.)

SO:

* Do your research. Fred heard about another passenger who had gotten a refund.
* Rules are meant to be questioned. It *said* in the brochure that there would be no refunds.
* Don't take no for an answer.
* Stay polite and persist. Persistence makes the difference. Fred had to ask three times.
* Businesses are worried about bad word-of-mouth. They know that negative publicity can lose them potential customers.

Would You Please Hold?

We're under siege from the long-distance phone carriers. I've said, "No, I'm not interested in switching" three nights in a row, told them not to call again, yet a few days later, received another call. And doesn't it always come when you're in the middle of discussing something important?

"Dear, I'd like to talk to you about our sex life—" Brrr-ring, brrr-ring.

Long-distance carriers are markedly self-serving and manipulative and have little interest in customer needs. That's why I play the "long-distance-service game." The game involves switching back and forth between long-distance carriers for bonus offers. To lure you to them or to retain your business, they'll give you cash, frequent-flyer miles, free air time, and rates lower than advertised. These bonuses are available without stipulation. I've made $300–$400 a year playing the switching game. Last year, it was close to $800 with two lines. There's nothing illegal or immoral about switching back and forth. The down-side is that it's time-consuming.

Some might find this practice nervy and out-of-line, but here's how I see it. They're at war for our business. And as the expression goes, "All's fair in love and war." They'll do almost anything to get it. *We* may be confused about appropriate behavior for dealing with business, but you can be sure they're not. If a friend calls every night during dinner to harangue us, we'd be shocked at the rudeness and lack of consideration, especially if we *asked* him not to call. We wouldn't expect such behavior from a friend, and we wouldn't exhibit such behavior toward him, yet the long-distance services feel free to call us every night with a sales pitch.

Repeated phone solicitations amount to harassment. Even an unlisted number doesn't stop them. My husband's number is unlisted, yet they feel free to violate his privacy at any time.

It must be that the companies derive some regulatory benefit for having large client rolls. Households are targeted on indicia such as sex, zip code, and annual income. What's puzzling is it doesn't seem to matter how much you spend. It's weird. Although my husband and I make all our long-distance calls on my line and use his for the Internet and the fax machine, the better offers come to him. His bill is about $5 a month and mine is closer to $100, yet he gets offered $100 to switch, and I get offered $50.

Then there's "slamming," where your long-distance carrier is switched without your permission. According to *Consumer Reports*, "this year and last, AT&T settled slamming charges in Florida and Texas for $800,000; paid Florida $240,000 in slamming penalties."[1] The Better Business Bureau receives more complaints about phone services than it does about any other business, including used car dealers.

Pay Now and Later

My friend Lucy is someone who doesn't like dealing with finances. It's almost as if there's something unclean about the whole thing. She hastily pays her bills without really looking at them. She paid a $24 bill from AT&T, though she vaguely thought she was now with MCI. The next month, when she received another bill from AT&T, she paid attention. The phone number for which she was being billed, she hadn't had in five years.

And long-distance phone companies lie. Recently, I've been told by three different MCI "associates" that mileage has been credited to my account; it never has. I've been told that it's 5 cents a minute on Saturdays and Sundays, when it's only 5 cents a minute on Sundays, and I've been lied to by omission—the nonmention of a minimum usage fee. I've had extra charges appear on my statements for services I never authorized—like $5 a month for an 800 number. I've been promised a $100 credit toward future phone bills which never materialized. When questioned, they've said they no longer send people checks, yet a week later I received a check for $100.

A huge source of revenue for the long-distance carriers is from customers who don't specify a long-distance carrier. If you don't choose one, you'll be assigned a carrier—whichever is the default carrier in your area—and charged the highest rates—$3 a minute. So even if you don't make many long-distance calls, be sure to designate a carrier or you'll be zonked with all kinds of outrageous charges. (Run and check your bills! You can get charges waived if you haven't been notified there's a penalty for not choosing a carrier.)

Add to all this, the fact that if you're a loyal customer, you won't be notified about lower-rate plans—and they're constantly lowering the rates. The low rates are to lure new customers, but you, the loyal customer will never hear about them unless you ask. It's like being charged full-price on a sale item in the supermarket because you haven't asked for the sale price.

And try calling them to correct problems. They, being the experts, have voice-prompted systems designed to drive the sanest crazy. They figure, and rightly so, that most people won't have the energy to challenge the lies, errors, and omissions. *And these very companies are counting on our applying the same rules of etiquette to them as we would to a friend.* When you cash the $100 check from AT&T, they're counting on your loyalty. They've bought you. They expect you to feel too guilty to switch.

So here's how the long-distance-service game works. MCI awards frequent-flier miles for switching—I've gotten as many as twelve thousand at a time. The offers are usually for five thousand miles, but sales people are authorized to award more. You have to ask. It takes at least a month to receive these miles—which forces you to stay with MCI while you wait. AT&T sends potential customers checks in varying amounts that, when cashed, switch you back to them. The only stipulation is that the check be cashed within thirty days. There are no requirements for a minimum period of use. In fact, one time, a check for $100 arrived from AT&T three days before I was moving. I cashed it, became a customer for three days, then signed up with MCI for bonus miles at my new phone number. These offers are, in a sense, discriminatory; they're *only* for a certain segment of the population. Those who Ask.

I call it a "game," because I've been known to get carried away with the challenge of it all.

SO:

- Long-distance phone companies use unethical, deceptive, and sometimes use downright dishonest tactics to get our business.

- You can benefit financially by their desire for our business.
- Don't pay a bill without looking at it carefully.
- When you move or get a new phone line, but sure to *specify* a long-distance carrier or your local phone company will assign you one and your long-distance bill will be astronomical.
- Operators have discretion. They can award you miles or lower your bill.
- Call phone companies during off-hours for better service.

A Tale of Two Ralphs

An assumption we make is that in the "old days" (translation—
sometime in the mythical past when we were young) things
were better. In respect to Customer Service, this notion
couldn't be further from the truth. In the "old days," it was difficult or impossible to return *anything,* even something new. Small
businesses wouldn't take anything back, and even department
stores gave you a hard time. At best, you could get a store
credit.

I was reminded of how bad things used to be by a recent experience with a dry cleaner—the words "dry cleaner," strike
terror in the hearts of most people—worse, maybe, than the
words "easy to assemble."

Well, this dry cleaner had business policies that harkened
back to the bad old days. They ruined our Ralph Lauren comforter that was part of a set I'd just purchased at Bloomingdale's.
It had taken ages to find a pattern that both my husband and I
liked. This was the one set that we both agreed on. I more than
liked it; I *loved* it. And not only had we found the right set, but
we'd paid an incredible price because the pattern was discontinued. Four pieces: a comforter, a dust ruffle, and two pillow

shams, all for $159. I soon learned the hard way just how incredible this price was.

The comforter handed to me by the cleaner was badly faded, and the filling so weakened there were hollow spaces in it. It looked like it had been washed in scorching water, but the manager insisted they'd washed it according to the instructions on the label. (That was interesting because there *was* no label. I remembered later I'd removed it and put it in my warranty folder.) The fault, he said, lay not with him, but with the manufacturer.

When I mentioned I'd washed the pillow shams and *they* hadn't faded, he repeated, in a bored and dismissive manner, that it was the manufacturer's fault. I could fill out a "discrepancy" report if I wished and leave the comforter three or four weeks for testing. No way. I had visions of the thing vaporizing into cyberspace.

Now comes the *good* news. Though this dry cleaner did business in the old-fashioned, pass-the-buck method, he was renting a space in a Supercenter, a large supermarket that housed other franchisers—a photo shop, a bank, a frozen yoghurt stand, a mailbox concession, a stationer, a café, and a bookstore. (These stores-within-stores are called lease departments. To draw the customer to the premises, large chains lease space to vendors with specialized services.) The supermarket, Ralphs, had a more contemporary, customer-friendly attitude than the dry cleaner. Another common assumption is that dealing with a small business is better—a kinder, more environmentally good thing to do. That may be the case sometimes, but often it's not. A big business has the resources to be responsive to the consumer, especially if it understands that keeping the customer happy is good business.

So my gut told me to cease dealing with this stonewalling

manager and take my problem elsewhere. I appropriated the "discrepancy" form and the comforter and left—without paying the $30 cleaning bill. No one rushed after me to collect the money, though it "wasn't their fault."

To determine the current prices, I went to a nearby department store, and told my sad tale to a saleswoman in the bedding department. I was hoping to enlist her sympathy and get some help. They had also carried the pattern, but not the king-sized set we needed. I asked the saleswoman if she could look up the original prices. But I'd knocked on the wrong door. This woman was a "stickler." It seems like every business has a few. You can spot them by their tone and officious manner. Nothing pleases them more than saying no. This stickler had no sympathy for my problem. They hadn't carried the pattern in two years, she said; and anyway, she wouldn't tell me the original prices because I'd only be reimbursed what I'd paid—all said with great conviction and hostility. I told her she was wrong; I'd seen the pattern there in the spring. At that, she bustled off, emanating fumes of outrage.

(Stay away from sticklers. They enjoy giving you a hard time. When you encounter one, give him or her a wide berth. Department stores allow their salespeople a lot of latitude, so take your items to another register—to a friendly salesperson, the kind who wants to help. The 20-percent-off coupon says you can use it on only one item; the friendly salesperson allows you to use it for five. You don't *have* a coupon? No problem. Ms. Friendly scans one she keeps in her register. She'll even *volunteer* that it's coupon time and whip one out.)

I decided to take bold steps to get what I needed, so I went over to the Ralph Lauren display and removed a pricing card. When I read it, I needed smelling salts. To replace what we had with something similar, we'd have to pay anywhere from $585 to

$720 depending on whether we bought something on sale. This was not a price range we were in.

That night my husband and I brainstormed the best approach. We could simply return the comforter to Bloomingdale's and they'd refund our money, but that didn't seem right. They weren't responsible. We decided, instead, that Ralphs was responsible. The dry cleaner was on their premises, and therefore, Ralphs should be held accountable.

Then we made another important decision—we giggled uneasily at the audaciousness of it, though we were convinced we were right. We decided *not* to volunteer our purchase receipt, but instead to ask for replacement costs. In the past I would have brought in the receipt, accepted reimbursement for the sale price—especially after the tongue-wagging I'd received from the stickler—and been grateful to get a refund. But $159 wouldn't go far at the current prices, not to mention the time we'd have to spend hunting for a new set. Only replacement costs would come close to making us whole.

The next morning I called the Supercenter, explained our problem to the manager, and asked for his help. He was totally sympathetic. In fact he said they'd had other problems with this vendor and were trying to get rid of him. (Not too reassuring for Jane Q. customer. Why didn't they put up warning signs?) The manager said he'd turn the problem over to the Property Management Department who'd "helped him out in the past."

My husband and I thought it was an excellent sign that the manager had "tipped us off" about other complaints he'd received. He'd offered a bit of information that worked in our favor.

A few hours later, when I hadn't yet heard from Property Management, I called the store manager again, just to let him know that I was *really* concerned. (Call early, call often.)

"Don't worry," he said. " 'Tracey' is working on it."

The next morning "Tracey" from Property Management finally called. She asked me to describe the incident to her. I started by mentioning that I was a good customer. She interrupted me.

"Yes, yes," she said, "Rick [the manager] made that perfectly clear."

They valued my business. *That* was nice. And they had an accurate accounting of what I spent because I used my "Ralphs Club Card." (You *have* to use it to get the sale prices, or you end up paying too much.) Stores gather a lot of information from these cards. They know what you buy, when, and how much. Here, however, it worked to my advantage. They *knew* I was a good customer.

Tracey asked me to complete the "discrepancy" form and fax it to her. I also faxed her the price list I'd picked up at Robinsons-May.

A day went by and I heard nothing, so I called Tracey in the late afternoon. She said she'd faxed the papers to the dry cleaner. Hadn't they called me? Was she kidding? Why had Ralphs handed the problem back to the dry cleaner? The optimism I'd felt when I first talked to the manager evaporated. No, they hadn't called me, I said. She'd call them again, she said.

A few minutes later I received a call from a person who identified herself as assistant to the president of the dry-cleaning firm. She wanted me to return the comforter so they could send it to the International Dry-Cleaning Institute in Pennsylvania for testing. Could I return it immediately? I refused. We were back to Square One.

Now I got agitated. Maybe it was time for the Big Threat— to take my business elsewhere, which I really didn't want to do. I *liked* shopping there. But I was exasperated. One more try before the Threat.

I called Tracey and told her I was putting the matter back into the hands of Ralphs, that I wanted *them* to reimburse me the replacement costs. *They* could go after the dry cleaner on their time, not mine. She said she didn't have the authority to make such a decision, but that she'd speak to higher ups and get back to me.

Not ten minutes later, the phone rang again. It was Tracey.

"Bring the entire set to the manager," she said, "and he'll reimburse you $720. We'll pass the costs on to the dry cleaner." I was astonished. Although the price card I'd faxed her contained both the retail prices *and* the sales prices, Tracy chose to reimburse me full replacement costs. Perhaps Ralphs was looking for ammunition to squeeze out a troublesome tenant, and our situation was useful to them.

I gathered everything up, rushed over to the store, and received $720 *in cash!* (They had me sign something. Probably willing over my firstborn, I don't know, I didn't read it, but she's an attorney. She can look out for herself.)

It was quite a high to receive the full replacement costs, and in cash. Though that's what we'd asked for, we'd never expected to get it. Some, like the Stickler, might say we weren't entitled to the $720, that we had "some nerve." But I felt good about *not* settling, about not volunteering what we'd paid. What you pay for something isn't relevant. What's relevant is what it will cost to replace it.

SO:

- Businesses are becoming more and more responsive to customer needs. Smart businesses know that it's good business to keep the customer happy.

* Larger businesses are often more responsive than small ones.
* If you're not getting satisfaction at the first level, bump up to the next.
* Listen carefully for tips that might help your case— "We've had other problems with this dry cleaner."
* You'll get better service from a business you patronize regularly.
* Call before writing.
* Call often, call early.
* Avoid sales people who are "sticklers."
* Be persistent.
* Don't let them distract you with forms and procedures. Tell them in clear, simple language exactly what remedy you want.

14.
Navigating Your Way to Good Health Care

This section is about getting the best medical care in our cumbersome health-care system, the epitome of asymmetrical, David and Goliath relationships. You not only have to ask to get what you need, you have to fight to get good medical care. You have to question, suggest, persist, do your own research, tell your doctor what to do. And if you're too sick to do it yourself, you need to get someone to do it for you.

Patients' Wrongs

Doctors aren't used to having their word questioned, and we're not used to questioning it. It takes effort. You have to push yourself. But in the current medical climate, with doctors pressured to see more patients in less time, unless you make yourself, what Bernie Siegal calls, the Exceptional Patient, you'll get care that's barely adequate.[1]

The recent horrifying report disclosing that medical error in hospitals causes between 44,000 and 98,000 deaths a year, means that it's crucial for us to take charge of our own health. Dr. Lucian Leape, M.D., a professor at the Harvard School of Public Health and contributor to the report, advises "do your own research, at the library or on the Internet. Ask what-and-where questions about every diagnostic test, every procedure, and especially about every drug."[2]

Linda Greider in an article in the February 2000 *AARP Bulletin,* writes about a phenomenon in current medical practice called the catch-23. According to the author, "the catch works this way: Doctors typically will listen to a patient's 'opening statement' little more than 23 seconds. . . . Doctors are under growing pressure to see many patients. . . . That means you, the

patient, must talk not only fast, but compellingly, even knowl-
edgeably, to get his or her attention. That's important for your
doctor to fully grasp what's bothering you. Too often doctors
don't. In fact, researchers are finding that one big reason treatments don't work—or aren't prescribed at all—is because of
problems in the way doctors and patients communicate. Or
more precisely, fail to communicate. And when communication
fails, the results can be disastrous."

She goes on to say that "medical authorities are coming to
the view that patients themselves must be more assertive in the
doctor-patient relationship. Studies show that doctors remember best the cases of assertive patients. **Medical outcomes
are also likely to be better.**"[3] (Bold, mine.)

We have to take charge of our own care. We have to train
physicians to meet our needs. I regard *myself,* not my internist, as
the overseer of my health. Medicine has become too complicated for internists to have more than surface knowledge, so if a
new health concern arises, I ask to be referred to a specialist.
And what I've found is that though the internist may have *discovered* the problem, the care you receive from a specialist makes
the internist look like a layman.

And when I'm seeing a doctor for the first time, I write a
letter detailing my symptoms and fax it ahead or hand it to the
nurse before she puts me in the cubicle. The letter accomplishes
several things. It gives you the opportunity to calmly think
through and describe your problem, rather than forget half of
what you want to say under the pressure of the doctor's office,
and it lets the doctor know you're an aware, informed patient.
Also, he or she can review your condition before walking into
the examination room. I bring along an extra copy to review
myself right before the appointment. Every doctor has been
grateful for this printed record. Something like the following:

Dear Dr.

I've been suffering with an eye problem for about three years, which has become more frequent in the last few days. I've been examined several times by ophthalmologists for this problem and they have found no explanation.

Up until now, once a month or once every other month, I would wake with a pain and tearing in my left eye which would last most of the day and disappear toward evening. In February 1999, I woke with this problem but also blurred vision in my left eye.

For the last few days, I've being having a continuous bout of a mild version of this problem: burning and a feeling that my eye is swollen even though it's not.

> *Thank you,*
> *Barbara Rollin*

(Interestingly, this was a situation where I needed a specialist within a specialty. Going to an ophthalmologist wasn't enough. The new doctor was a cornea specialist and knew exactly and instantaneously what my condition was—corneal erosion. Three other ophthalmologists didn't have a clue or even think to send me to a specialist. This is the condition for which I need the saline drops. He said it was very common. Maybe in *his* office. I've never heard of anyone else with this condition, except maybe the actor, Albert Brooks, who used a saline solution in the movie, *Out of Sight*.)

Also, I bring a micro recorder to doctor's appointments. Tact is important in introducing this "ear" into the examining room. Some doctors flinch when they see it—as if I've taken out a gun.

"Would it be okay," I ask, "to use this recorder so I won't miss anything you say? It would be really helpful."

At a first appointment, I ask the doctor for her callback schedule—so I don't have to sit by the phone. A solution to phone sitting is getting a cell phone and listing it as your primary number. Also, I ask for the doctor's fax number and E-mail address. Further, anytime I have worrisome symptoms and have to wait for test results, I ask the doctor what the odds are that I have something serious. Usually, the possibilities are much less awful than what I'd conjure up on my own.

And persistence is essential. It can take exhaustive effort to penetrate the many layers to get the care you need. Often doctors don't get messages, nurses don't call back, test results get lost. Keep calling. Write yourself reminders. If you don't receive a timely phone call, call again. Stel was told she needed hip surgery—a good thing too because she could hardly walk—but there were no openings for a month. Stel freaked. The month would be thrown down the drain because she was in constant pain and couldn't work or enjoy anything. She called the doctor's office and enlisted the aid of his nurse.

"Please," she said, "I can't wait a month. I'm in too much pain. Can you do anything to get me in there sooner?"

Stel was operated on the next day. Because she asked.

If you're very ill, bring along a relative or a friend. You'll be too frightened and distracted to hear what the doctor says, too frightened to ask the right questions or make decisions. I have an agreement with a few friends and, of course, my husband, that we'll accompany each other to serious medical appointments at *any* time. Three o'clock in the morning, two o'clock in the afternoon.

In hospitals, too, you can get help from a patient advocate.

It's not that the doctors don't care. According to a recent survey of "169 internists in eight cities . . . 58 percent considered it ethical to lie for a patient who needed a heart bypass operation, and 48 percent considered it ethical to lie to get intravenous pain medication and nutrition for a dying cancer patient. The percentages were lower for less serious conditions."[4] (No face-lift fibs.)

That being said, many doctors don't think outside of the box. When my husband's ninety-year-old father broke his hip, there were all sorts of complications like congestive heart failure, infection, loss of swallowing reflex. Yet four days after surgery, the doctor said he was stable enough to go to a nursing home.

"Are you sure he's ready to be moved?" my husband asked.

The doctor immediately said, "Maybe I can get the insurance company to authorize another day." Another day didn't change things. What we didn't realize was that the nursing home was totally inadequate to deal with my father-in-law's condition. This we found out the hard way—he died three days later. In retrospect, it seems obvious he should have been kept in the hospital longer—much longer—but the doctor didn't tell us that, he only said that insurance wouldn't pay for any more days. Why didn't he give us the option to pay for the hospital ourselves? Because it never occurred to him that we'd be willing to pay. He assumed that if insurance wouldn't pay, the man *had* to be sent to a nursing home. This doctor didn't think out of the box.

I had a similar instance with boxed-in thinking when I changed insurance plans and had a bone-density scan under the new plan. The scan the previous year had shown some bone loss—a condition called osteopenia—and on the advice of my previous internist, I'd been taking Fosamax, in *addition* to hormone replacement therapy to build bone mass.

I asked, and had been assured by the technician, that the current equipment was the same as the one used in my previous scan; but when I called my internist to get the results, the nurse said the technologies were different and the results couldn't be compared.

"Continue the Fosamax and we'll retest you next year," was her breezy advice. Just like that, stay on an expensive medication that has annoying side effects for another year. That wasn't good enough. *I* needed to know whether I had built up bone mass even if the nurse wasn't interested.

I called the previous year's lab to determine if they still used the same equipment and to ask what it would cost to have another test. The equipment was the same and for $150 I could find out if I really needed to continue with the medication, or if it was doing any good at all.

Even monetarily, the doctor's attitude didn't make any sense. A year's worth of Fosamax would cost me $140. It would cost the insurance company $300. Why hadn't my doctor suggested another scan? She probably hadn't thought of it. Or maybe she wanted to avoid doing extra work. She'd have to get approval for a second scan. Yet I was willing to pay for the second scan.

If you feel another test should be ordered and insurance won't cover it, consider paying yourself. At the very least, it will buy peace of mind, which, in my opinion anyway, is well worth paying for. In fact, I'm convinced it's critical to put the doctor on notice, in writing, that you're willing to pay for *any* test, treatment, or care that would be beneficial **even if it's not covered.**

A short history of medical insurance in this country will explain why doctors don't like to suggest any procedure that isn't covered by insurance. Fifty years ago there *was* no medical insurance. The doctor came to the house—a house-call was $5 or so—you gave him a cup of coffee and some homemade cake.

Then came medical insurance which covered *everything*. Copays were low and you could go as often as you liked to as many specialists as you liked. People grew accustomed to a cradle-to-grave medical security blanket. Then came Managed Care, with its gatekeepers and accountants and everything changed.

We felt as if something was being taken from us—as, in fact, it was. Uneasiness and distrust of the medical profession seeped into the common consciousness. In this climate doctors try to avoid patient outrage by staying in the box. It's rare for a doctor to recommend a procedure not covered by insurance. They don't want to hear a patient ask, "If you're recommending this, why won't insurance cover it?"

More on the Fosomax story. Finally, after prolonged attempts to get some attention from the lab and my primary care physician (I've since left her "care"), I decided to refer *myself* to an osteoporosis specialist. He *was* able to compare the two scans and said I was being overmedicated and should discontinue the Fosomax and take only the hormone replacements. (It's been my experience that specialists medicate *less* than internists because of their detailed knowledge of the latest developments in their area and their greater understanding of the risks and benefits of specific medications.)

I tell this story to illustrate how you have to be your own doctor, not take the information you're given at face value, but press on for more help. Nobody can care for you the way you can care for yourself. No one else has as much at stake. And trust your gut. Don't let that surgeon operate if you don't have good feelings about him or her. Get a second opinion.

An important benefit of taking charge of your health is, you won't feel helpless in the face of problems. You won't have to add anxiety and depression to other symptoms because you'll feel empowered.

SO:

- You have to take charge of your own health.
- You have a right to ask any questions of your health-care providers.
- You have to fight, persist, research, ask, to get good medical care.
- Become an exceptional patient. Doctors and their staff will remember you and you'll get better care.
- Get thee to a specialist.
- Bring a tape recorder to important medical consultations.
- Pay attention to your gut.
- Fax or hand your doctor a letter detailing your symptoms.
- Find out when the doctor does his callbacks, who's his nurse, his fax and E-mail addresses.
- Persist.
- If you're ill, bring someone with you.
- Let your doctor know that you want *any* procedure that he deems necessary, even if insurance won't pay.

Conclusion

Around the time I was finishing this book, I had coffee with a new friend, Esther, a writer and professor of feminist theory. Esther was very interested in my book and asked me a lot of questions.

"You mean," she said incredulously, "if you've gotten a cup of coffee that's cold and a little weak, you can ask them to give you another cup?" Like most of us, she was bold and confident in some areas, and not in others.

"Absolutely," I said. "Is *your* coffee too weak?" She'd been working on it for ten minutes.

"Yes," she said, sheepishly.

"Why don't you ask them for another cup?"

"What do I say?"

"Just ask them for help."

I watched as she went up to the counter, smiled apologetically, and asked for some help.

"No problem," the young man behind the counter said. "We just made a fresh pot." He removed her cup and gave her a new one filled with steaming coffee.

She came back to the table beaming. She was actually thrilled by her success—and amazed that a simple, direct request could reap such an easy solution.

This was as big a victory for Esther as my financially successful ones were for me.

What is *Ask!* really about and what does it mean for you? It means you have the power to better your situation in a way that's effective and psychologically healthy. It means you can reduce the everyday stresses in your life and free up time for more productive and enjoyable activities. It means you can financially recoup from formerly losing situations in a manner that's good for you *and* good for the businesses you deal with.

Sometimes behaving differently doesn't feel comfortable at first. It feels unnatural and wrong. After a while, though, new behaviors become more and more comfortable and require less effort.

You have to choose your priorities. You might decide not to return anything under $5. Or under $20. You might not want to make more than one set of phone calls, or spend more than half an hour on a problem; but the important thing is, *you* get to choose.

Appendices

Annoying Business Practices

* Businesses that don't have liberal return policies.
* Their warranty policies are onerous, i.e., they insist you keep the original packaging.
* It takes days for them to return your call.
* Although they have 800 numbers, you're put in a continuous loop—voice-mail-jail—and it takes too long to speak to a live person. I've run into this a lot with computer tech "support." They give you an estimate of your wait, sometimes in the *double-digits*. Telling a customer their waiting time is twenty-four minutes is surely a way to discourage that customer from ever calling again.
* In calling about your phone service or your credit card, they make you punch in your phone number, credit card number, an automated voice verifies, then when you finally do get a live person, they ask for the number again. It's no mean feat to keep reading off credit card numbers. And there's no reason to do so. The way technology is today ". . . systems are capable of transmitting customer records that have been scanned into a computer system to a particular customer service representative *while the phone is still ringing into the customer center. . . .*"[1]

+ They can't help you right now because their "system is down." Get a new system!
+ Salespeople who say, "We don't," or, "We only." Why not stress the positive. Tell me what you *have,* not what you *don't* have.
+ Salespeople in shoe departments who say, "We don't have these in a size seven, but we have a nine and a half black." Well maybe I'll grow into them.

What's Worked for Me

- Keep receipts for at least a year, including sales tags.
- Check your credit-card statements to be sure you've received credit for your returns.
- If you're expecting something in the mail, or, a return call, force yourself to wait before pursuing it. It usually shows up the next day, and you've wasted a lot of time. If possible, force yourself to wait three days.
- Doesn't every piece of alarming mail appear late Friday or Saturday so you have to spend an uncomfortable weekend? You can't wait till Monday to call. But don't. Don't make complaints, inquiries, etc., on Monday, for obvious reasons. It will be unproductive and frustrating. The rest of the world is also waiting to pounce on the phone Monday morning.
- Get a speaker phone. You can do all kinds of paperwork while waiting for the music to stop and the hard-to-catch person to pick up. Don't think you can leave a message and have them call back. You'll have to wait it out on hold if you want to get your situation addressed so you might as well write some checks or even go back to your breakfast coffee.

+ Keep a list of all those you need to hear back from either by phone or mail and refer to the list daily.

+ "When you make a complaint, keep a record of phone calls, dates, and notations. Get the first and, if possible, the last names of all the people you deal with." We hear this advice all the time, but often it's pretty hard to follow. Sometimes you don't even know something is going to turn into a problem, and you haven't kept *any* names. Follow through anyway. Often, it doesn't matter, especially if the business knows it's in the wrong.

+ Try to get yourself to ask for and repeat the name of *anyone* you talk to in a business transaction, even if it's a small one like requesting a catalogue, even if you don't actually write the name down. It keeps employees on their toes, alerts them they might be held accountable. Many times when I *haven't* asked for their name, I *didn't* receive the catalogue.

+ Most voice-mail systems still give you the option of holding for an operator if you don't have a touch-tone phone. Pretend you don't have a touch-tone phone. It can be the least frustrating way to negotiate the system.

+ Shit-Happens Emergency Fund—You lock your keys in your car, you back your car into a pole, a tooth breaks. Here in sunny Southern California, they make the parking slots about a foot narrower than in the East. You can count on dent-and-run bumper damage at least twice a year. And no one graces your windshield with a note of apology or a phone number.

Expensive, inconvenient, depressing, annoying, and guaranteed to occur on a regular, random basis. Count on "throwing away" $500 to a $1,000 a year—and that's in a *good* year. I try to think of it as a regular expense—like food and shelter.

The Principles of Ask!

* If it doesn't satisfy, take it back.
* "Rules" are meant to be questioned.
* If you don't understand jargon, or haven't heard what someone said, don't be embarrassed, force yourself to "Ask."
* Find out what the return policy is. If you don't see it posted, Ask.
* Specify what remedy you want.
* Be persistent. Call three days in a row. You'll get some attention.
* Don't present for inspection.
* Go right to the top.
* Time is money.
* Know when to fold.
* Do your homework.
* Calling is better than writing, showing up in person is even better.
* You'll get better results from a merchant you deal with regularly.
* Don't settle for less than you think you're entitled to just because you're grateful to get *something*.
* A first offer is just that—a *first* offer.
* Get names and phone numbers of everyone you talk to. Repeat the name often during the conversation. This accomplishes two things:

(1) it creates a more friendly, personal atmosphere, and (2) it lets them know you *know* their name and they will be held accountable.

* Stay courteous. I try to get into a mind-set before I make any call that these people are on *my* side. I'm calling to enlist their help. They'd really like to help if I'm courteous and don't put them on the defensive. "I wonder if you can help me." "I hope that I can get some help." "I'm a little confused about my last bill, I wonder if you can help . . ."

* Ask the merchant to put himself in your place. "Put yourself in my place. How would you feel if you had to wait two extra hours?" "How would you feel if you paid for something you never got?"

* When you receive unsolicited sales calls, just say, "This is not directed against you," and hang up.

* If you're thinking of purchasing something for which you'll need technical support—try getting ahold of the support staff by phone or E-mail *before* you purchase the product, and base your decision on how easy this is to accomplish.

Notes

CHAPTER 1: IF YOU DON'T ASK, THE ANSWER IS ALWAYS NO

1. Martin E. P. Seligman, *Learned Optimism, How to Change Your Mind and Your Life* (A. A. Knopf, 1991).
2. See *Why We Buy* by Paco Underhill (Simon & Schuster Trade, April 2000), for an idea of what businesses know about our shopping habits.
3. *Consumer Reports,* "Food Fight," September 2000, p. 13.

CHAPTER 2: ASKING—THE HOWS AND WHYS

1. Jennifer S. Lee, "Addition to Consumers' Arsenal: Net Complaint Services for Hire," The *New York Times:* Technology (July 8, 1999), p. 140. Quoted from article in *A Complaint Is a Gift,* Janelle Barlow and Claus Møller (Barrett-Kohler Publishers, 1996).
2. Wade, Betsy, "A Flier's Guide to Complaining," The *New York Times,* Practical Traveler, March 12, 2000, p. 4.
3. Bryan A. Garner, "What's the Plural of Mouse? 'Wired Style' Says 'Mouses,'" *The San Diego Union-Tribune,* ComputerLink, March 14, 2000, p. 5.

4. Michael Stetz, "He Gets Kicks in Kooky Queries to Companies: Man's Offbeat Letters Lead to Laughter, Book," *The San Diego Union-Tribune,* December 27, 1999, p. B-1.
5. Ibid.
6. Ibid.

CHAPTER 3: FINDING HELP WITHIN THE SYSTEM

1. Janelle Barlow and Claus Møller, *A Complaint Is a Gift* (Barrett-Koeller Publishers), p. 37.
2. Ibid., p. 24.
3. Ibid., pp. 24–25.
4. David Horowitz, *Fight Back, and Don't Get Ripped Off* (Harper & Row, 1979).
5. Ellen Phillips, *Shocked, Appalled, and Dismayed* (Vintage, 1998).
6. Elinor Burkett with Frank Bruni, *Consumer Terrorism: How to Wage War against Bad Products and Worse Service* (HarperTrade, January 1997).
7. John Bear and Mariah Bear, *Complaint Letters for Busy People* (Career Press, Franklin Lakes, NJ).
8. Dave Murphy, "Do Happier Airline Employees Make Flying Safer for All?" *San Diego Union-Tribune,* Travel Section, February 27, 2000, p. 5.

CHAPTER 5: GETTING OVER YOUR SHAME OF RETURNS,
OR, MANY HAPPY RETURNS

1. Randy Cohen, "Milking Mr. Softee," The Ethicist, The *New York Times,* February 20, 2000.

CHAPTER 6: RETURNING SERVICES

1. *The Holiday Inn Hospitality Promise* brochure.
2. Edwin McDowell, "Best Western Aims at Corporate Travelers on a Tight Budget," The *New York Times* (April 18, 1999): Business Section.

CHAPTER 7: ASKING SERVICE PEOPLE FOR HELP

1. Janelle Barlow and Claus Møller, *A Complaint Is a Gift,* p. 25.
2. Ibid., p. 200.
3. Anthony Robertson, "Pudding Plus Persistence Equals a Really Sweet Deal," The *Sacramento Bee,* January 27, 2000, p. A4.

CHAPTER 11: ASKING TO BE TREATED FAIRLY

1. *Consumer Reports,* "Food Fight," September 2000, p. 16.
2. *Consumer Reports,* "Food Fight," September 2000, p. 13.

CHAPTER 12: ASKING FOR THE INFORMATION YOU NEED

1. Seff, Marsha Kay, "Traffic Alert: Disclosure Rule May Include Clogged Freeways," *The San Diego Union-Tribune,* Homes Section, February 27, 2000, p. 1.

CHAPTER 13: DOING GRADUATE WORK

1. *Consumer Reports,* "The New Phone Tug-of-War," July 1999, p. 8.

CHAPTER 14: NAVIGATING YOUR WAY TO GOOD HEALTH CARE

1. Bernie S. Siegal, M.D., *Love, Medicine and Miracles* (HarperPerennial, 1990).
2. Linda Greider, "Beware of Catch 23: Talking Back to Your Doctor Works," *AARP Bulletin,* February 2000, pp. 3, 25.
3. Ibid.
4. Brenda C. Coleman, "Doctors Say Fibbing for Patients OK," *The San Diego Union-Tribune,* Monday, October 25, 1999, p. 2.

APPENDICES

1. Janelle Barlow and Claus Møller, *A Complaint Is a Gift,* p. 142.